THE

"WHAT DO YOU MEAN I'M IN CHARGE
OF THE SCHOOL PAGEANT?"

HANDBOOK

D1537105

By

JOHN CARROLL

EDITOR
Frank Alexander

ARTIST
Dawn Bates

Published by FRONT ROW EXPERIENCE, 540 Discovery Bay Blvd., Byron, California 94514

500 BOOKS IN PRINT AS OF 1987

Published

by

FRONT ROW EXPERIENCE
540 Discovery Bay Blvd.
Byron, Calif. 94514

This book is dedicated to

HAL

Who deserves a Standing Ovation

ABOUT THE AUTHOR

John Carroll has survived producing, directing and writing dozens of children's plays for schools, recreation departments and camp groups. His involvement in children's theatre includes working for various city recreation departments, teaching creative dramatics for all ages from 3 year olds to senior citizens, as well as teaching theatre arts at the high school level for several years.

As a published playwright, John has written for adults as well as children and his plays are produced throughout the United States. They include "Oh, What A Tangled Web", "If It Don't Hurt, It Ain't Love", "Murder Well Rehearsed", "The Enchanted Bicycle", "The Marvelous Machine" and "The Folks Next Door" which was optioned for a television movie of the week. He has also written the books to the musicals "Ship Shapes" which opened in Los Angeles and "Babes In Barns" which played in Chicago.

He received his B.A. in English from Loyola University in Los Angeles and attended Schiller College in London, the University of Nairobi in Africa and the American Academy of Dramatic Arts. He is currently pursuing his Masters Degree in Education.

TABLE OF CONTENTS

ACT ONE

(Introduction)

Hey, I understand! You don't have to apologize to me for missing the P.T.A. meeting last night. Sure, your kid was sick and the dog threw up on the carpet and your mate couldn't find the remote control unit for the TV and besides, well, you did promise your mother you'd finish the book she lent you. I understand how something like a P.T.A. meeting could slip your busy mind.

Then, isn't it nice to have good friends like Veronica Volunteer who, in between making cookies for the boy scouts, fighting to save the seals and working as vice president of three civic organizations, will take the time out of her busy schedule to come and inform you that in your absence at last night's meeting, YOU were nominated to direct this year's school pageant, "A Salute To Radishes".

Undoubtedly, she will tell you that the committee voted you as director because you are so creative. What she actually means is that no one else volunteered. But she stood right up and said that you would make the best director since Cecil B. Who-ever.

You? A director? You who don't know a stage lamp from a stage coach? You who thinks great acting is Miss Piggy? You who thought "thespian" was something not mentioned in polite company? You? A director of an entire school production?

OK. Now that we have the panic out of our system, let's get working. Let's start with a couple of basic rules:

      RULE ONE: RELAX

      RULE TWO: Stop laughing hysterically about Rule One and do it. It really isn't as difficult as it looks.

Putting on a production, be it a Broadway hit or a third grade production of "King Lear" (with all the "dirty parts" cut) can actually be fun.

Yes, fun.

And lest you think my idea of fun is somehow associated with wearing leather restraints and hitting my head against the wall, I have found that working with children to put on a production is a rewarding although tiring challenge.

(My therapist told me last week that I can start working with real people again soon.)

Thus, this book. To help you over the mistakes that I have made putting together a zillion children's productions (actually, it only seems like a zillion).

You will find, hopefully, the answers to your questions on children's theatre, costumes, sets and several threats and scowling looks to give when all else fails.

Advance towards this mission as you would any civic project. **Order** is the first order of the day. Without order, you will have chaos.

With order, you will have ordered chaos. But at least you will know where the catastrophe is located. This doesn't help much, but as the sets start falling, the children begin kicking the lighting technicians and the opening night programs have been locked in your uncle's car, you can point with pride and say: "Look how organized I am. I know exactly what is going wrong!"

Chapter 1

"WHAT'S A NICE PERSON LIKE ME DOING IN A THEATRE LIKE THIS?"

(You Become A Director)

CHOOSING A PLAY

Undoubtedly, if you missed the P.T.A. meeting when you were nominated as director, you also weren't aware that the committee had also chosen a play for you to direct. You will find that the universal characteristic of such committees are that:

A)   They lack imagination in choosing your epic.

B)   They choose a play that is technically the most difficult to produce ("The Ten Commandments as a musical would be nice").

C)   They have absolutely no theatrical interest and just want to get their children off the streets and into tights.

It is up to you, therefore, to cope with some of the bizarre suggestions that come up. Undoubtedly, if you have a group of fifteen boys and three girls, the committee will suggest "Little Women". Conversely, if you have forty-five little girls and two boys (which is always the case) they will suggest "Tom Sawyer".

After you hear these crazed people out, quietly go about doing your homework. Try to pick out a play that you like. After all, you will be living with it for about 10 weeks (and reliving it each time you run into one of your stars at the mall). If you get ill at the sight of Julie Andrews, for gosh sakes, steer clear of Mary Poppins. If the idea of another revival of "The Wizard Of Oz" leaves you off the yellow brick road, try another path.

Do not, repeat, DO NOT choose a play simply based on the cartoon version you enjoyed at the age of twelve. Your chances of getting that script are not too great.

Before you even start bantering titles around, there are several things to take into consideration.

1) CAST SIZE

Do you know approximately how many children you will be working with? Is it a club or a class that you are dealing with? Will everyone be expected to be in your stellar production or can you audition for the best darn actor in Akron for the role?

You should have a pretty good idea of the interest level of the group you are working with. Doing a pint size production of "Gone With The Wind" is not needed when only six kids have responded to your cry of "Let's Put On A Show!"

2) LENGTH

How long is this epic going to run? Best not go over an hour, especially if this is your debut as a director. I find the ideal length to be anywhere from fifteen minutes for tiny youngsters to an hour for preteens. I would be willing to go an hour and a half if the school choir sang before and you promised an intermission. Folding chairs and grammar school auditoriums are always uncomfortable and cold. Have compassion on parents who just got off a full days work.

3) BUDGET

How much is the committee, school board, group willing to spend? (In a nutshell, this will be as little as possible, I can guarantee you.) If there is no budget, you may have to rule out royalty plays (plays that charge the group for production) or plays with elaborate sets and costumes. Best to find out early how much money you are dealing with before being told you are over budget and the life sized toy soldiers have to be replaced with cardboard.

4) COSTUMES AND SETS

Doing the play "The Wizard Of Oz" sounds like a sure fire hit. But do you have any idea how difficult it is to come up with a "Tin Man" costume in size 6? And Ruby Slippers are not the easiest thing to find in mother's closet. While searching for a play, keep in mind that your little kiddies are going to have to wear something besides their "Star Wars" T-shirts and tennies.

And also be aware of the number of set changes involved. No matter how exciting your pageant on Columbus may be, no one wants to wait 10 minutes between scenes while the sets are changed. You may want to start small with a show with one or two sets. Be wary of plays that have more than three set changes in them. It will put a strain on you and your stage crew.

5) TIME

Think about it. Do you really have enough time to do a huge production? If you are approached on December 1 to do a production of "A Christmas Carol", gracefully bow out. It is a long process and one that should be thought out at least 3 months before production dates.

6) LOCATION

Where is this extravaganza going to be held? Is there a stage? Is there seating or will your audience be on the floor? (Not a popular choice for grandmas.) Is there a backstage area for your actors to wait? Will you be rehearsing on the stage itself or some other area until the actual performance? It really shakes kids up to rehearse one place and put on the show somewhere else. They suddenly become fascinated with their shoelaces, the only familiar thing around, in the middle of your production.

7) TECHNICAL DIFFICULTIES

Will Peter Pan have wires and be able to fly around the stage? Can you get a witch to melt? Can you find a Santa Claus suit in July? How will Alice get through the looking glass, the prince fight a dragon or an entire village materialize? These are a few problems you should think about while reading scripts. Can you do it, with a little help of your audience's imagination? Be wary that many children's plays are difficult to translate from book to stage. Look for these problems. They are not insurmountable but do require a few tricks to get over them.

8) MUSICAL

If all the above were not enough, someone, probably our old friend Veronica Volunteer, will come up with the sterling suggestion of doing a "musical comedy". In itself, not such a bad idea. In many cities, the yearly musicals are a big draw.

However, remember your budget and time load. Musicals are much more expensive in everything from royalties to sets.

Also, let's face a few facts. Although you may look great doing the "Hustle" at Bob and Grace's Bar-B-Ques, you will be the first to admit you are not Bob Fosse. (He's a choreographer.)

And if you are the type that has trouble playing chopsticks on the piano unless someone points out "C" (that's "do" to us musical geniuses) I would strongly suggest you shuffle off away from a musical.

However, if the idea of a musical means a few songs stuck into the script, this can be a delight. And if your musical expertise can be summed up in three words ("Just Sing Loud"), and you don't worry about the critical aspect, then by all means, change Red Ridinghood into a musical.

Remember, you are dealing with children. They love to sing by themselves and do frequently. But the idea of singing before an audience may be intimidating. Make it fun for them too. So they may be off key. At least they are trying.

You will find people who actually write songs in your community. Use them if they are simple (the songs, not the people!). Use old standard songs or incorporate a few "pop" songs into the show. (The kids will know them!)

Perhaps your choir teacher has a few outstanding pupils who won't throw up at the mention of stardom. Use them as well. Use the teachers and anyone else you can get your hands on. Make it fun and light and everyone will have a good time.

You may want to use smaller children to sing a song or two. (Munchkins? Merry Villagers?) Just be sure you rehearse how to get them on and off stage.

These mini-musicals can be a lot of fun. Be wary of royalties you may have to pay for the use of certain songs and be creative when choosing songs. Also, be aware that having a twelve year old boy who is going through changing vocal chords sing a sopranic version of "Climb Every Mountain" may not exactly be everyone's idea of a musical highlight. Keep the songs simple and in low keys for all the children.

9) WHY?

The big question is saved for last......Why are you doing this show? Let's face it, if your goal is to raise a quarter of a million dollars for a burn unit at your hospital......Lots of luck! No one makes a big profit in children's shows. (Don't believe all those Mickey Rooney-Judy Garland movies where they take their shows to Broadway and save the orphanage, buy the band new uniforms and still have enough to save old Widow Carstair's barn from the bank.)

However, if you are looking at this as an educational experience, I can promise you that it will be just that. More for you than the kids, perhaps, but all in all......It will be an experience.

These are just a few of the major questions you should raise whenever one of your friends gets that "Show-Business-is-my-life......Let's-do-a-play" look in her eyes.

If, by some lucky chance, you are free to choose a play without committees and helpful parents, never fear. After hours of pouring over play catalogues, revamping the third act, and finally coming up with the ideal play meeting all requirements for budget, casting and sets, your lead actor will probably tell you the first day of rehearsal "This play stinks".

Just keep repeating to yourself "Child abuse is not legal in this state.....Child abuse is not legal in this state....."

Chapter 2

A PLAY, IS A PLAY?

(Searching For The Ideal Script)

You've narrowed the field down. You want to do a simple Christmas pageant with maybe a few dancing snowmen and perhaps a hint of Dickens. The play committee wants you to do the unabridged version of "The Nutcracker" even though no one's child has ever had ballet or even knows what a nutcracker is.

Not to worry. You've done your homework and presented your case. Win or lose, you have reached SOME decision on the type of play you, your committee and your budget can live with. Now where do you find your script?

ROYALTY PLAYS

There are several leading publishing houses that deal exclusively with plays. (A list follows this chapter of play publishers and addresses.) The majority of these plays will be royalty plays (no, not about kings and queens!). That simply means that the publishers work with the author and there is a charge to the producers of the play each time it is presented.

Do not think that just because you are not charging admission to the Grant Avenue Junior High School version of one of these plays that you do not have to pay royalty. Check out the rights and payments of the play publisher early on.

And don't even think of duplicating a copy of a script and not paying the royalties. Authors make their livings off royalties you pay. (That is, everytime the play is performed you pay "X" amount of dollars which the publisher and the author split.) You will be paying for more than just the scripts.

Most royalties run between $5 to $15 for a one act, $20 to $50 for a two act of moderate success. Musicals run sky high with royalty being based on the number in attendance. Royalties are due before the play is performed so make sure that whatever the cost is, you have it budgeted.

Send away to the publishers for a list of their plays. They will send you a catalog that will give brief summaries of their shows, how many characters and sets there are and the cost of each script and the royalties for each performance.

Don't be surprised that there are several versions of old favorites. There are quite a few Tom Sawyers, Cinderellas, Snow Whites, etc. Make sure you don't just pick one. Try to read each version and see which fits your cast, budget and staging requirements. Some may be too adult for your kiddies, others may have too many set changes. Read them carefully.

Send away for the scripts that interest you. They usually cost between $2 to $4 for a copy. (Keep your receipts to present to the budget committee!) As you read them, see if you can visualize this play being done with your group. Are there any difficult sets involved? Is the dialogue easy enough for your age group? Are the parts equally divided? Is it fun for you, the children and the audience?

WHAT TO LOOK FOR

There are hundreds of so-called children's plays out there. Unfortunately, many of them stink. (Hey, I've written a few klunkers myself so I can talk.) Either they talk down to the children or are written so gut wrenchingly cute that the audience suddenly goes into insulin attacks before the second scene. Many of them do not spread the parts out evenly so you are stuck with having two or three children carry a scene while the merry villagers all but disappear into the backdrop.

Read a few plays. Become accustomed to them. Several new plays are very funny and well written, dealing with contemporary problems. Many are written for adult actors to perform for children. Choose one that is comparable with your sense of humor and style. Remember, you are an adult and if you like it, chances are so will your audience.

EXAMPLES

A BAD SCRIPT FOR YOUNG ACTORS

PRINCE: Oh Cinderella, you are the most ravishing woman at this gala. Your eyes are like tiny pools of water that reflect the love I feel for you at this very instant. Oh, promise me that we may dance every gavotte at tonight's festivities? Please, my darling?

CINDERELLA: In truth, fair Prince, I must be honest and warn you that when the clock doeth strike the midnight hour, I must flee to the safety of my abode.

PRINCE: Oh, I dare not blink for I may wake and find such ecstasy but a dream.

A BETTER SCRIPT FOR YOUNG ACTORS

PRINCE: You look nice.

CINDERELLA: Thank you. I'm happy to be here.

PRINCE: Want to dance?

CINDERELLA: Sure but I have to be home soon.

OK, OK. So maybe I am laying it on a bit thick. But plays like the first example do exist. They expect kiddies to understand words of more than two syllables and leave it up to a director to explain what the #*%&$ these words mean. The second example gets the plot moving and gives more chances for other actors to come in and give a line or two.

Be aware of the vocabulary of most scripts. Some may be over the heads of your young actors. Read with a teacher's eye and see if you can make changes to have the play fit your needs.

But never fear.

After changing all the big words for smaller words, after finding a script with equal lines for the children, and after adapting the play to fit your physical needs, those lines you slaved over will either be forgotten or not heard by the parents sitting in the cavernous auditorium.

But hey! That's show biz.

PLAY PUBLISHERS

Most publishers will send you a list of their plays.

PUBLISHER	DESCRIPTION
BAKER PLAY PUBLISHING 100 Chauncy Street Boston, MA 02111	Large collection of children's plays and amatuer shows. Noted for large selection of religious plays.
CONTEMPORARY DRAMA SERVICE 885 Elkton Drive Colorado Springs, CO 80907	Specializes in "Readers Theatre" and elementary material for church/school.
DRAMATIC PUBLISHING CO. 311 Washington St., P.O. Box 109 Woodstock, IL 60098	Large selection of plays for adults and children. Lots of adaptations here.
ELDRIDGE PUBLISHING CO. Drawer 216 Franklin, OH 45005	Primarily deals with amateur groups with plays for all ages.
SAMUEL FRENCH INC. 25 W. 45th St. New York, NY 10036	World's largest publisher of plays. Mostly publishes Broadway shows. Large Children's selection.
PERFORMANCE PUBLISHING CO. 978 N. McLean Blvd. Elgin, IL 60120	Large selection of plays for amateur groups. Teen comedies and musicals especially good.
PIONEER DRAMA SERVICE 2171 S. Colorado Blvd. Box 22555 Denver, CO 80222	Good selection of plays for high school and elementary.
PLAYS MAGAZINE 120 Boylston Boston, MA 02116	Great introduction to theatre for teachers and students. A monthly magazine with plays for all ages. No royalties if you subscribe!

Chapter 3

NEIL SIMON, EAT YOUR HEART OUT

(Write Your Own Play?)

So you've done your homework. Your kitchen table is strewn with playscripts from every imaginable publishing house. You have waded through four dozen versions of "Sleeping Beauty", sixteen "Tom Sawyers", five "Holiday Pageants" and several that all seem to blur together and you still have not found the right script for your group.

This is especially true with regards to holiday shows. You have four teachers with a class of twenty kids each all wanting to be in your Easter Bunny salute and there's only six parts in "Peter Cottontail".

What's a director to do?

Well, before I offer the next suggestion, I seriously advise you to keep an open mind, a smile on your face and hide all sharp objects. Are you sitting down? Good. Then here's my suggestion.

Why not write your own?

(I can hear you laughing out there!)

Oh, sure, I've heard it all before. How your fingers get caught in the typewriter keys and you can never remember how to spell "proscenium" and besides, Miss Williams who taught creative writing at your high school suggested you switch to shop. Sure, sure, sure. But doesn't it appeal to you in a perverted way?

You, the Tennessee Williams of Keeokuk, Iowa!

By writing your own script, you can adapt it to your needs, your cast, your stage and your budget. (Who says there are only seven dwarfs? When you write it with your Girl Scout troop in mind, it could be 16 dwarfs. And Cinderella doesn't have to go in a pumpkin coach if your budget won't allow. Just have her take the bus!)

It also gives you a chance to put in local and topical humor. (Although I have found out that principals and group leaders do not relish having the "Big, Ugly Troll" named after them! The kids, however, love it!)

WRITING THE PLAY

If you decide to write your own play, don't get all involved in your creative endeavor and forget that there will be an audience out there. Remember there are parents who just put in a hard day at the office and want to be home watching Monday Night Football. Let's not overkill them with a musical salute to salt in seven acts and 34 scenes.

Take a look at a few of those scripts that are laying all over your kitchen. Basically, it has the characters name and what he or she says. That's it.

Even you can do that!

Don't be afraid to be daring. Take the basic outline, if you are doing a "classic" and keep all the "have to do" scenes (Snow White and the apple, Red Ridinghood and the Wolf", etc.).

Now, try it from a different slant. Writing your own play helps you stamp out the awful violence and sexism in children's stories. Remember, some of these stories are eons old. So why limit yourself? No one has to die. The wolf in Red Ridinghood can reform and be sent to a zoo in California. The Wicked Witch in the "Wizard Of Oz" can be shrunk in the water, or better yet, learn the beauty of personal hygiene. And what's wrong with having a "Tin Woodsperson" or a Lioness in "The Wizard Of Oz".....or "The Wizardess Of Oz". And the "Empresses' New Clothes" can be just as fun!

Help stamp out the sexist remarks or ethnic slurs that still cling to children's literature.

Be creative with naming your characters. The fairies in "Sleeping Beauty" can be named "Eeeny, Meenie, Mynee and Moe". I always enjoy plays with a "King Stuffshirt" and "Queen Bea" and kids eat up on these silly names. In fact, having them help name their characters can add to the fun.

Don't be afraid to put in a few "groaners". (That is, jokes that elicit a groan of recognition. Example: Alice is amazed that Wonderland has talking flowers. "Of course we can talk" says one of the flowers. "Haven't you realized that we have Tulips?" Get it? "Two lips?" Yuk, yuk, yuk. Sure it's corny, but it still gets a laugh and sometimes a groan of appreciation.)

Writing your own also give you a chance to put in a few songs or specialties. You have a tap dancing virtuoso? By all means, have the Blue Fairy do a tap solo. Someone juggles? Sings songs? Whatever, you can incorporate this very easily.

GETTING HELP

Kids are natural story tellers (just ask one sometime how the kitchen window got broken and settle back for a story that would make Mark Twain envious). If time permits, how about a group adventure in writing? Take their ideas and incorporate them into your story.

Be warned, however, that this can become frustrating. You may sit down with a group of kids, pen poised for the ideal Christmas fantasy and find them staring at you as if they were posing for a still life.

Conversely, you may get a precocious child who is destined to become the next Neil Simon come up with the ideal plot, characters, setting and expound on this in great length, leaving the others in the cold.

If you do consider this group adventure, try to do it in a classroom-type situation and help them discover their own potential imaginative stories.

However, be wary when they come up with the most perfect story line and you race home to spend hours typing it up only to have a spouse read over your shoulder and on page 16 say "Oh, yeah. I saw that last night on "The Cosby Show".

So what? Shakespear stole plots too, didn't he?

Writing your own play is fun.....Really! But be flexible. Kids are hams and may not say the lines the way you wrote them. (Perhaps not even in the order you wrote them.) But remember, this is a creative venture. Sitting on little Sally and telling her that unless she says "What HO, the PRINCE!" instead of "WHAT HO? The prince?" that she will never work in theatre again is not creative!

Chapter 4

"I DID NOT STUDY WITH LEE STRASBERG FOR AN ENTIRE SUMMER SO I COULD FOLD PROGRAMS!"

(Staffing)

Success! You have chosen a play. This after Vernonica Volunteer insisted on "Goldilocks" (Need I tell you what color her oldest girl's tresses are? Hmmm?) And the head of the committee felt that "Carmen" with second graders would be a real challenge.

Whatever play you have chosen, be it royalty versus writing your own, while the scripts are being readied or ordered, NOW is the time to get organized. Now without the hint of audition in the air. Now, while parents are still fired up. Now, while you can still make it through the night without those recurring nightmares of twenty little children staring at you with eyes straight out of "Children Of The Damned".

Now is the time you should start thinking about your staff. Don't be afraid of that word. I don't expect you to run out to an employment office and hire a full time clerical staff. I do expect you to surround yourself with people who will help you cope with the project that is before you.

YOUR STAFF

It's a natural mistake for beginners to want to do it "all themselves" even at the price of a job, a marriage or their sanity all for the love of "the theatah".

They are the ones who write the play, direct it, make the scenery, do the costumes, work the lights, pass out programs on opening night, give the cast party and obtain a full head of gray hair in just three weeks just so when someone says "Harv, you did a great job" they can say "Oh, it was nothing" before visiting hours at the rest home are over.

Following is a list of people you may or may not need for your particular production. I will explain their jobs in the real theatre and you may find you can get by with combining a few of the jobs. Remember, you want help in this production, but the last thing you need is a group of volunteers who don't do anything but help their own kid to shine.

If you decide you want to do it all by yourself, ask yourself "Do I really want to be left alone with twenty-three sweaty, untrained children for a couple of hours a week?"

If you're human, you'll look over the list again.

ASSISTANT DIRECTOR

An assistant director, even if it is just a high school student or someone slightly older than your cast, is a joy, a blessing, a gift to be looked upon as manna from heaven.

That is, only if he or she is a **good** assistant.

If they aren't, it's like being on the Titanic with only one way to go.....DOWN!

Choose your assistant with care. You will be spending a lot of time together.....Especially at the corner bar after rehearsals. A good assistant director (or "A.D." as they are known in the biz) is one who:

A) Works well with you

B) Works well with children

C) Is creative

D) Does not know the meaning of the phrase "I know it's **harder,** but why don't we do it this way....."

Your first impulse may be to grab your best friend and corner them into doing it.

Remember, friendship is a delicate thing. Do you really want to risk losing a good friend in order that your school can have the "best darn Arbor Day Show"? Think it over.

What can your assistant do?

Oh, ye of little faith! A good assistant can help you move mountains.

First and foremost, an assistant will be good for traffic control, if nothing else. Let's face it. When faced with thirty hostile kids the first day of rehearsal, it's not so intimidating if there is someone else there who is over four feet tall and can speak without the accompaniment of snapping bubble gum.

An assistant lets you direct while he/she is wrestling with Bobby who refuses to put on tights and "bloom" as a rosebud. An assistant can play creative games like, "Who can be the quietest cast member the longest", while you go over Harold's one line ("Hark") and explain his motivation.

An assistant can watch that the bees don't cross pollinate while you are battling the set people over a mauve Plymouth Rock. The assistant can keep track of the blocking (where the kiddies are suppose to stand and move on stage) and keep the kids off the sets when they are not suppose to be on stage. An assistant should come with a ton of creative games and stunts that require no props and are very, very quiet.

Now that you finally admitted you need help (I hope!), don't go overboard. Limit your assistants to what you truly need. Often times, a group of parents will swear that they want to help out and either never show up or just sit at the rehearsals and become a bother wondering why their Sonny doesn't have all the "good" lines. Better to have a non-partial assistant than a mother who mutters throughout.

PIANIST/ACCOMPANIST

If you are planning on putting music into your show or just want to have music between the scene changes (a blessing to a poor audience stuck in the dark——it gives them a chance to listen to something besides a frustrated stage hand dropping a paper mache tree stump on his foot), a pianist who likes kids is a joy to have around. Putting music into plays is fun and most kids love to learn songs. (NOTE: Don't force the little darlings to learn "The Major General's Song" from "The Pirates Of Penzance" or an operatic aria. Nice simple little tunes are fun. ANOTHER NOTE: If you ever AND I MEAN **EVER** tell a child that he or she has a lousy voice and they better "just move their lips while the others sing", I will personally come to your house late at night and do horrible things to your prized petunias!)

Add a few basic dance steps and you can have a mini-musical. (More on this later.) If you can get a good pianist, nab them. Get the music to them early so they will know the score (neat pun there) before the first rehearsal. Have them work with some kids teaching them songs while you work with others blocking the scene and your assistant works with another group painting scenery.

See how it works?

COSTUMER

If you are going to have a fairy tale play or a "Salute To The Wild West", you are going to need costumes. Parents love costumes because they make all those pictures they take at the performance "cuter". Kids love costumes because it gives them something to play with while on stage. You can love costumes if you have a good costumer who can coordinate it all.

Most plays for children take place "Once Upon A Time" and for some unknown reason, this means medieval times to everyone. So it's time to drag out mom's old formal and dad's bathrobe for the queen and king's costumes. All the townspeople must be dressed in color coordinated tights and the evil Duke must, of course, have a big black cape.

For the sole purpose of hanging these things up after rehearsal, you need a costumer!

A mom or dad who sews is a blessing. A costumer should be on board early to take measurements of the actors as soon as possible. Do not wait until a week before and go to the poor parent who checked "I am interested in helping with costumes" on your survey and tell them you need 400 mice outfits for "The Pied Piper".

You may never work in theatre again!

Make sure you and your costumer have the same idea as to what the costumes will look like and what the budget will be. (Sequins and rik-rak add up! Try to be creative and simple at the same time.)

Don't let your costumer get carried away.

TRUE STORY TIME: When I did a high school version of "The Sound Of Music", the costumer, a well meaning mother, spent four weeks making Maria's wedding dress. It was an authentic-looking 1940 silk dress that Maria wore for exactly 14 seconds in the play to walk from one side of the stage to the other. Granted, it was a beautiful moment, but at the dress rehearsal with the show opening three days later, I asked where the rest of Maria's costumes were. The mother shrugged but again expounded on the beauty of the wedding dress. A quick call to the local German restaurant and a deal with the owner to let us use his waitresses' dirndls netted our Maria her first three costumes!

So be careful! Keep an eye on the costumer and know your budget and time allotment and make sure that they do too!

SET DESIGNER/SET BUILDER

It always seems that the scenery is unthought about until the day before the play when you suddenly become aware that there is no Ebeneezer Scrooge's house!

THIS IS A NO-NO!

Sets should be designed before the rehearsals begin so that the director will be able to warn the little darlings that they won't be able to dance off stage right because there will be a forty foot beanstalk there. Again, turn to mothers and fathers who are handy with hammers. Sets should be constructed of light material, but sturdy enough to stand up when a well meaning frog accidentally bumps a tree.

Given a choice of the two, I think parents prefer great costumes to great sets for the simple reason they are looking **for** Little Susie and not for a two story dwarf's house that has running water and windows that really open.

TICKET SALES/PUBLICITY MANAGER

Are you selling tickets to this extravaganza? Get one of the parents, who is a business man or woman, involved and stay clear of that area of theatre. It is a royal pain.

Keeping track of the pennies and nickels that come in is impossible when your sleeping beauty snores and the sets are falling down. Using precious rehearsal time to collect money, distribute tickets and keep a tally of how many seats are still unsold is not a creative process for a director of your stature.

DELEGATE!

If you are going to have tickets, make sure you keep a tight control over how many are printed. Do not print a thousand if your theatre only holds fifty-seven. And specify the dates the tickets are to be used for. If you have a three right "run", more than likely everyone will show up on the Saturday night. Tell your ticket chairperson to be aware of this.

A publicity chairperson is important if you are looking for outsiders to attend your show. Someone who can write a press release, bug the local newspapers for coverage, take photos and make posters is wonderful. They too are sometimes overlooked until a week before the show. (Most newspapers ask for two to four weeks prior notice for press releases. They don't print them on demand, no matter how creative you are with your threats.)

A ticket person and publicity person can be one and the same, if you are worried about finding bodies. The two go hand in hand for each must know what the other is doing in order to do the job the best they can.

STAGE MANAGER

A stage manager is the one who makes sure everything that is suppose to happen on stage, happens. Many opening nights have been ruined as the director yelled, "places", the actors scrambled to their spots and.....NOTHING HAPPENED! Because they forgot to assign someone to pull the curtain.

A stage manager makes sure the props are in place, the sets are moved, the curtain pulled and everyone is in the correct place. His favorite expression is, "Quiet backstage". A stage manager allows you to stand out front with the audiences, smiling as he or she wrestles with a stage frightened goat in "Heidi".

LIAISON

You may need a buffer to act between you and your committee and you and the parents of the young actors. This is someone who will fight your battles for you for more money, take parent's phone calls when they call to complain their little darling deserved the lead, work with a clerical staff to type programs, etc., etc. This could be a group leader, a principal or recreation leader, depending on what group you are working with. It is always nice to have someone "in the front office" that is aware of what you are trying to do and will help out in an administrative capacity.

HOUSE MANAGER

I know, I know.....We all need one of these. Unfortunately, this one doesn't do windows or balance your budget. This is the person in charge of everything that happens in your auditorium. They must be responsible for the box office, making sure there are enough chairs set up, programs, ushers (if you use them), punch and cookies served during intermission (although, you can have a separate "refreshment" chairperson), air conditioning, and making sure the place is unlocked before the audience arrives and is locked up after they leave.

This job doesn't require a whole lot of time and many parents should latch onto this one as the "easy one". Don't discourage them. Let them find out that searching for the auditorium keys at midnight is no joy.

Depending where your play will be performed, it is not inadvisable to make sure the House Manager has access to a large, strong looking parent or associate. Sometimes, rowdy kids need to be "escorted" out of the auditorium or the basketball team may arrive to practice during the opening number. It doesn't hurt to have a large adult say in basso profundo, "That's show biz", as they move the offenders out.

MAKE UP CREW

Mothers love this job. They get a chance to go backstage before the show and make their little darling look like a refugee from "The Rocky Horror Show". Be warned! Given a tube of lipstick and a little rouge, some mothers love to obliterate that natural charm of your lead and make the play into a surreal nightmare of brightly painted red lips and deep mascara-ed eyes.....And that's the Prince!

Children are not thrilled by makeup. It smells. It feels funny and it smears. Try to get by with as little as possible. Since you are hopefully not working with lighting that will rival any New York theatre, it is not necessary to go into great lengths for everyday makeup. A bit of lipstick and rouge is fine for the girls. If you want ruddy looking boys, have them run around outside before the play.

You will need a makeup crew for special makeup like Hansel and Gretl's witch. This is fun. Choose a parent who is a bit artistic and carefully explain what you need. Remember, no matter how special the makeup is, deep down inside, every parent wants to see their child up there. Why hide all the face? Suggestive makeup is more fun for the makeup crew, the audience and the kid.

LIGHTING DIRECTOR

A lighting crew is great to have, but only.....(AND THIS IS INCREDIBLY TECHNICAL, SO BEAR WITH ME).....Only **if you have lights.** Most children's plays have such intricate light plots as "The lights come up" at the beginning and "The lights fade" at the end. In most theatres or playing areas your production will be running, this will mean a flip of one switch. In this case, it can be done by the stage manager.

However, if your playing area does have lights (professional or just spotlights), you will need someone to aim them and make sure the areas you want lit are lit. This is not a demanding job, unless it requires re-hanging all the lights. You can get by with a parent who wants to volunteer but doesn't have much time. They can do the lighting in one day.....UNLESS you are doing special effects or creating your own lights (see chapter on lights) in which case you must once again weasle your way into the hearts of good natured parents and whine until the job is done.

Granted, you may not have any friends when the show is done, but at least no one will ever forget the year "Who's-its directed the show".

CLEAN UP STAFF

And isn't this always the plumb job? Beg, steal or borrow someone who will volunteer to help put away the folding chairs, mop up spilt punch, clean up the dressing rooms and put everything back to normal before the spring break. It always seems that school pageants are held right before vacations and YOU certainly don't want to be putting away chairs until midnight and miss the better half of the cast party!

Those are the basics. You can elaborate if you wish with a Musical Director, if you are having the chorus sing, a choreographer, if your kiddies will dance, ushers, wardrobe assistants, makeup crew, etc., etc. Do not try doing it all yourself! (Have I repeated that enough?)

BEATING THE BUSHES

What's this? Suddenly Veronica Volunteer has no time for this production (which was her original suggestion)? She throws you a three hundred page synopsis of "Gone With The Wind" and says, "Order me three tickets for opening night", and is off to "Save The Whales"?

OK, don't panic.

On second thought, do panic and get it over with. Then roll up your sleeves and decide to do the best play you can without killing yourself. If it is too late to turn around, charge ahead. Just go easy on sets and costumes. Figure out the simplest way to do it with minimum risk to health, marital status, or mental capacity. Kids have a great imagination and it is contagious. Before you know it, your audience will believe that the curtain is the door to the Prince's castle and that old evening dress sheared down is really a ballroom gown.

Send out flyers before you start casting, seeing if there is parental interest and what kind. Give them a chance to choose where their hidden talents lie. When all you get back is a reverberating silence, wait until after you have cast the play and send another flyer out with the children in the show. Use that wonderful trick of the trade.....Guilt! Let the parents know that you certainly don't mind spending your afternoons with their child (thus relieving them of day care costs), and wouldn't it be nice if they repaid you by a few, small, insignificant hours of work on the production.

"Blackmail is such an ugly word, my dear.....Let's just call it 'theater'."

Try sending out something like the following:

Dear Parent:

As you are aware, our annual Holiday Show is drawing near. (DON'T BE SURPRISED IF THEY ARE NOT AWARE SINCE JUNIOR PROBABLY LOST THE ANNOUNCEMENT. GIVE THEM THE VITAL INFORMATION AGAIN.) This year, our fourth, fifth and sixth graders will be presenting "Holidays Around The World" on December 14 and 15 in the Cafetorium.

This show will be bigger than our Christopher Columbus Pageant. (START BUTTERING THEM UP HERE.) Your work on that show made a tremendous difference and the children still talk about it. (THOSE WHO SURVIVED!)

I realize how busy the holiday season can be, with shopping, cooking and decorating.....(START LAYING THE GUILT HERE).....but I am sure you realize how important it is that the children learn the true meaning of the holiday season.

(ZING IT HOME HERE) Attached, please find a list of backstage assignments we are looking toward the parent's to fulfill. Please check the area(s) you have skill in and return it no later than October 15. Our first meeting for backstage staff will be November 1, so mark your calendars now. (DO NOT OFFER THEM A CHOICE. THEY WILL SIGN UP, THEY WILL ATTEND THE MEETING, THEY WILL HAVE A GREAT TIME. PERIOD.)

Thank you for your help. I look forward to working with you again!

RETURN BY NOVEMBER 1 TO BILLY'S HOMEROOM TEACHER

Parent's Name_____

Phone_____

Child's name and class_____

I can help in the following area (Check as many as you feel comfortable doing)

_____Set design

_____Set construction

_____Make up

_____Clean up Crew

_____Assistant Directing

_____Musical Directing

_____Traffic Control

_____Program

_____Ushering

_____Ticket Sales

_____Publicity

(LIST AS MANY ASSIGNMENTS AS YOU THINK YOU WILL NEED, DO NOT WORRY ABOUT OVERLOAD. YOU WILL BE LUCKY IF FOUR PARENTS RETURN THESE! ALSO, DISREGARD ANY OBSCENE MESSAGE SOME PARENTS MAY SCRAWL A-CROSS THIS. AFTER ALL, IT IS SHOW BIZ!)

Chapter 5

"WHERE ARE MICKEY AND JUDY WHEN YOU NEED THEM?"

(Budget)

In all those old M.G.M. musicals, when someone leapt up and suggested putting on a show to save the orphanage, not once did some bespectacled kid stand up and say, "Excuse me but have you worked out a budget for this extravaganza?" Oh, sure. Mickey Rooney may have gotten in over his head once in a while, but then Judy Garland, the daughter of the bank president, was always there, feeding his ego and paying the bills "for the good of the show".

It ain't like that folks. You're going to find that even the simplest of productions must have a budget.

Gone are the days when Jo Marsh hung up the drapes in the living room and did her seven act romantic dramas in "Little Women". Today you have royalty payments, set rentals, costumes and even cookies and punch to contend with.

Your committee will probably welcome you aboard with open arms and empty pockets. When you are offered this choice position as director, make one of the first questions out of your mouth be, "What's the budget?"

This will be met with usually loud silence as the members hem and haw. Press them for a bottom line figure.

If they are expecting you to do a mini-version of "Nicholas Nickleby" (only 3 hours long as compared to Broadways 8 hour version) and give you a grand total of twenty-five dollars, smile broadly and get the heck out of there.

You cannot expect a play to rise from the ashes. Now is the time to budget how much you will need for your show.

THE BUDGET

First of all, how much is YOUR time worth? If you are volunteering, that is fine, but if you are to get a "honorarium" (translation: a pittance), find out how much it is first. It won't be worth half of what you are, but what the heck.....This is show biz. Consider it paying your dues.

However, if you are doing it purely as a volunteer, then make sure you don't LOSE money doing it! Expect a budget for your production and do not pay for anything out of your own pocket! Tell the committee how much you will need to put on the show and stick to it.

After your own worth, how much will be available for "the help"? For those parents who are helping out in a big way such as building sets and making costumes, will there be any money? Will they be volunteers also or will they receive stipends? How much are they worth to you?

Materials are expensive so how much will your costumer need to put together a "Salute To Ragweed" number for your fourth graders? How much will music cost? Program printing? Cookies for intermission? YOU SHOULD NOT PAY THESE YOURSELF!!

Sets are expensive to make and to rent. Wood costs money. So do nails, hammers, saws, paint, cardboard, cloth, bolts.....(Are you getting the idea?)

Be prepared to go before your "producers" with a list of expenses. Here is a checklist you and your production team might find helpful in computing your expenses.

BUDGETING YOUR PRODUCTION

SCRIPTS
Cost per script
Cost of duplicating scripts
Royalty payments of scripts
Postage for scripts

COSTUMES
    Materials (cloth, scissors, thread, needles)
    Rental of costumes
    Buying of costumes
    Costume Designer salary
    Costume Staff salary
    Dry cleaning costs

SETS
    Materials (paint, wood, tools, etc.)
    Rental of sets
    Staff salary

CHOREOGRAPHER
    Records/tapes
    Salary

MUSICAL DIRECTOR
    Sheet music
    Duplication
    Salary

PROGRAMS
    Photocopying
    Typing

PUBLICITY
    Posters (include money for paint, cardboard, etc.)
    Gas money for distribution
    Photos (film, development)
    Press Release duplication and stamps for mailing
    Flyers (cost of printing and distribution)

SOUND
    Rental of speakers, record players, etc.

LIGHTING
    Rental of lights
    Replacement of bulbs, etc.

THEATRE
    Rental
    Clean-up

REFRESHMENTS
    Cookies/punch for intermission
    Punch bowl
    Paper goods (cups, forks, table cloth)

STAFF
    If your staff will be paid, what is the fairest means of compensation?

MAKEUP
    Supplies
    Staff
    <u>CLEAN-UP</u> materials

I am sure there are hundreds of other items that your specific theatre group will need, but this will give you an idea.

Remember, there are TWO words to the term, "Show Business". So many people get caught up in the first (SHOW), they forget the second (BUSINESS).

You will find that Veronica Volunteer has forgotten about the small detail of budgeting in her fervor to get Veronica Junior on the stage. You should not be expected to shoulder the financial burden yourself.

STICKING TO YOUR BUDGET

Once you have figured out exactly what you will need to produce your show, STICK TO IT! Oh, sure. You read in the paper all the time where a major motion picture is ONLY 3.5 million dollars over budget and still goes on to become one of the highest grossing pictures in history.

REMINDER: YOU ARE NOT SYLVESTER STALLONE!

You must keep within your budget!

Theatre gets a bad reputation for this very reason. A school board or group committee will give you a small budget and it is up to you, at the beginning, to realize what you can do for that amount. To repeatedly go back to beg for more money makes group leaders very upset. Especially when you bring a ten year old in a half done costume and say, "Can you turn down little Jill here just when she has learned the essence of her character as 'The Troll'."

If the budget is not enough to cover what you foresee as your expenses, go to the committee then. Explain your plight. If it falls on deaf ears, reevaluate your thinking, simplify your expectations and make some cuts. Perhaps instead of full makeup, a bit of rouge will do. Costume corners can be cut and perhaps you could get the printing volunteered. Look around to (gulp) the parents once more. (I promise, after three or four years, they will stop running away from you when they accidentally bump into you at the market.)

DONATIONS

Ask for donations of items or money. Old clothes make great costumes. A lot of mommies have old lipstick that is just gathering dust in drawers. Perhaps someone manages a print shop for tickets and programs. Anyone in the lumber business?

Do not hesitate to trade with local merchants. Free advertising in your program allows you some bargaining power. (Although, you and they both know that precious few people will pick up the "Maple Avenue Sixth Grader's Salute To Spring" program when looking for a building contractor. But what the heck? It elevates what you're doing from "begging" to "trading business services".)

Do not start rehearsals with no budget and think that once ticket sales come pouring in you will pay back everyone. No, no, no. First of all, ticket sales do not come "pouring in" until the night before the show in which case the finance company has probably come to take your sets and costumes away.

Second of all, you may not be charging for this production. Make sure you follow what the committee has outlines. In many cases, charging admission is frowned on.

I also do not relish the idea of having fund raisers for the show unless it is done months before rehearsals start. It divides your energy, running from rehearsal to home to bake four dozen cookies and then out to a fund-raiser at night.

Be aware of your budget. Make friends with it and it will take care of you. Cross it and you will be eaten alive!

But, hey! It's only money.

Chapter 6

"LIFE UPON THE WICKED STAGE"

(Parts Of The Stage)

So, there you sit, smiling contentedly. You have your script. You have your staff. You have your budget. You are now ready for the onslaught.

But wait! Now is the time to do a little homework so when a third grader asks you, "But what's my motivation?", you don't answer, "Because if you don't do it, I'll see you never work in this town again!"

You have been a marvel at organizing it all and are proud of your self for all the preproduction work you have done. However, now you are expected to direct the entire thing!

There you are, facing your stage. Be it a cafeteria floor, a real stage with no wings (no, not the kind that fly) or just an open area, this is where your show of shows will take place. You are responsible for everything that goes on up there.

Intimidated?

A wee bit perhaps, but there is nothing frightening about an empty stage. No matter, where you will be performing, all theatres have the same logistics. Once you master one, you got them all.

The theatre, be it a community hall or a Broadway legit house, has several parts you should know. Let's start by dividing your theatre into thirds': The House, The Stage, Backstage.

THE HOUSE

The house is simply where the audience sits. It can be as elaborate as three balconies or just thirty rows of folding chairs. Although your attention is primarily on the on-stage activities, be aware of your audience throughout the rehearsal process.

Will all seats be able to see the action you are directing? Many new directors get the wonderful idea of putting some action on the main floor of the auditorium, off the stage proper. They reason that this action can be done while the sets on the stage are being changed. Nice idea, but if you have ever sat on a folding chair behind some-one who should be playing for the Laker's you know that no one past the first two rows will see little Billy and Julie do their big scene.

Your primary interest in directing is making sure everyone can see your play or better yet, can take photos (since that seems the parent's main objective).

Lay out your house so that there is plenty of room between rows. Add cushions, if there are folding chairs. Be aware if there will be air conditioning or not (making it impossible to hear little Charlie's, "To Be Or Not To Be", speech). Are there windows that will allow sunlight in, thus ruining your scary "Haunted Forest" scene? Is the "house" on the gym floor and will the coach be upset that there are four hundred folding chairs on his floating court? Will he allow hard sole shoes on it?

When setting up the chairs, remember that parents will be leaping up and down to take photos. Be aware and allow space. You may also want to allow little brothers and sisters to sit up close to the stage and you can put down pillows or low benches for them.

The house is also the place where tickets are sold, programs handed out, refreshments served, etc. Some of the lights may be in the house, but are handled from backstage.

The house should be clean and appealing since it is the first indication of the type of show you are doing. Posters out front, drawn perhaps by your young actors, can make it appealing.

THE STAGE

For some reason, the stage always takes on a mythical sort of quality. Everyone wants to be "up there" in the spotlight, but so few know anything about it.

Let's assume you have a real stage with curtains and a raised platform. (This is a big assumption for many groups. If you do not have a real stage, do not worry. I will be brief.)

OK. Here are a few terms that may help you. There is no reason for you to memorize these. There is little reason for you to even know these but sometimes they pop up in scripts. It is best to understand these in case someone's parent who worked for Sandy Duncan's brother-in-law says something technical. You won't have to look at them blankly.

So here goes. (No, you will not be tested later.) (See diagram on page 32.)

PROSCENIUM ARCH - The opening that frames the stage and separates the stage from the house.

MAIN CURTAIN - The curtain that hangs from the proscenium arch.

TEASERS - The horizontal part of your curtains.

TORMENTORS - The curtains that are on the side of the arch.

BACK WALL - The back wall of the stage. (Isn't this easy?)

WINGS - The area on either side of the stage behind the proscenium arch where the actors wait to go on.

FOOTLIGHTS - The lights at the foot of the stage.

RIGGING/GRID - What are you reading this for? You are evidently planning some huge major production, if you are even contemplating using grids or riggings! OK! OK. I'll tell you. They are the catwalks above the proscenium arch from which sets are flown in (dropped in on wires). But why are you looking up there? Are you entertaining ideas of grandeur on your first outing? Come back to earth.

THE THRUST - This is the part of the stage that is in front of the closed curtains. Many scenes can be played here as long as it is elevated above audience eye level.

THE PIT - ("Orchestra Pit") - The area in front of the thrust into which no normal active child can resist jumping. This should be your first threat! "Do not jump into the orchestra pit! If the fall doesn't break your legs, I will!" (Honestly, officer, I love kids!")

The stage itself is easily divided into areas which make it easy for the director to move his actors and scenery around. Check out the diagram on page 33. Intriguing, is it not? It shows you a typical stage aerial view. If you note, center stage is, cleverly enough, the very center of the stage. When you move left or right, it is always from the viewpoint of the actor looking out into the audience.

In other words: When you are standing in the House (see how these terms pop up?), your direction will be backwards. When screaming to little Jamie to go to stage left,

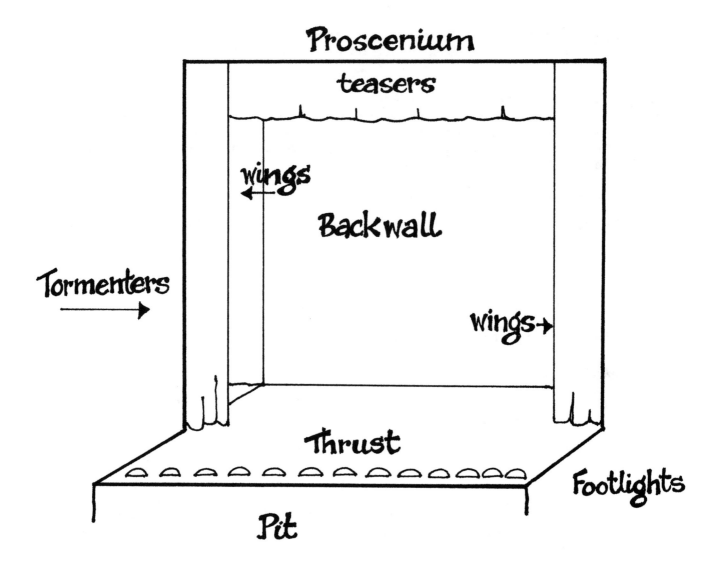

it is HIS left, facing you, NOT YOUR LEFT!

Sound too technical? Besides, little Jamie may have never learned left from right and you aren't about to mess him up with stage left and stage right. Let me give you an easy out. God bless America, for almost every school auditorium or cafeteria with a stage has flags. The State flag is usually always stage right and the American flag is usually always stage left. Use this bit of information.

Tell the children to "exit to State flag" or "Go towards the American flag side". No flags? Use other boundaries. ("Go towards the windows", if a row of windows line one side of the theatre.)

Use colored chalk to mark each side ("Go to the green side."). Or hang banners, use the wall with the clock, anything that will give them a sense of direction.

Your script will be loaded with "Amie exits UCL ("up center left") and you do not have to follow them. Your set may not look like the one that the author is suggesting, so your Amy could exit "blue side of curtain on wall clock side".

UC
UR   *upstage*   UL

stage right   CR   *center*   CL   *stage left*

downstage

DR   DC   DL

House

TERMS

UR – Upstage Right	DC – Downstage Center
R – Right of Center Stage	UL – Upstage Left
DR – Downstage Right	L – Left of Center Stage
UC – Above Center Stage	DL – Downstage Left
C – Center Stage	

BACKSTAGE

If yours is a typical school or group's stage, the backstage area will be nonexistent. There will be no room for storing sets, making up actors and having any type of crew members congregate. Of course, you took this into consideration when selecting a play and do not have a show that has the Nina, the Pinta, and the Santa Maria all sailing off stage left.

If you are lucky, you will have room in the wings for actors to stand waiting for their cue. In most cases, however, there will be a door that will lead either outside or to a hallway. Use this. In fact, use as much space as you can beg, borrow, or steal. (Isn't theatre fun?)

You will need backstage areas for dressing rooms. Hopefully, you will not have to have coed dressing rooms or will not have use of the bathrooms for changing. It is very disheartening for a child to be dressing into their butterfly costume while the audience is trooping in to use the facilities.

You will also need an area for makeup. Try to get this away from the waiting area. Trying to draw a moustache on a hyper child as his friends egg him on is not good for the makeup artist's ego.

A waiting room ("Green Room", as it is called on "The Johnny Carson Show") is a place that the children can wait until it is time for them to go on.

This room should be close enough to the stage so they can make it on cue and far enough away that parents in the first four rows of the audience don't hear the giggling and laughing that is bound to go on. Having a supply of quiet games and books, as well as enough water and snacks to keep the kiddies quiet, is essential. No matter how much you threaten, they will be as hyper as you have ever seen them so make sure there is plenty to keep them busy.

Backstage is also where your sets are stored. Before you design a seventy-five foot Plymouth Rock, make sure there will be a place to store it backstage while the first scene is going on. (NOTE: Please notice how big the doors are in your auditorium when thinking of your set. I have know way too many productions that have designed seven foot sets only to find the doors are six foot.) Props need storage space also. Try to find a place that you can lock your props into after each production, especially if you are sharing the facility with other groups.

Make sure there is enough adult supervision backstage and limit the number of people who are allowed back there before and after the show. Make sure you have a safe place for the kids to leave their clothes and valuables. (A beat-up baseball card of He-Man may not seem valuable to you, but just you wait until it turns up missing!)

Sometimes your dressing rooms, waiting areas and set storage will be far from the stage. Make sure you have parents in each room to watch your little hams. Do not leave the little darlings in a classroom unattended, no matter how angelic they look in their little costumes. You may come back to find your lead actor has loosened a screw from a lightswitch and stuck it up his nose (don't ask.....). Although an ambulance arrival does add excitement to your production, it is sorely out of place for "Little Women".

CHECK IT OUT

Make sure you see your playing area prior to going into rehearsal. You may want to be aware of any problems that exist. Are there other sets on the stage? Will other groups be using it? Are there any sharp objects that protrude off the wall backstage you should be aware of? Do the curtains work?

Do not accept the job and expect to walk into the theatre the day before the show and have it sparkling. Who will clean the place?

Find out what your keys will and will not open before the first rehearsal. Do you have access to the bathrooms during rehearsals? To the wardrobe? To the lights? Check this all out before your young cast stands there, watching you fumble with seventy five keys, looking for the one to the "Boys" room.

NO STAGE

What's that?

You say your school doesn't have a stage? That there are no lights? No folding chairs? No storage space? And they STILL expect you to put on a prize winning production? What, you scream, should you do?

Are you a religious person?

Actually, a lack of stage can present interesting challenges to you and your cast. (Oh, migosh, I'm beginning to sound like a school administrator!)

My first words of warning on this matter is don't even think of doing a play "in the round" (that is, the stage on the cafeteria floor with seats all around it). Kids have enough trouble with the audience in front of them. To make them be surrounded by the enemy ("parents") is too much.

If you are doing it in the gym or the cafeteria, make sure either the audience or the stage is elevated. A gym usually has bleachers so the action can take place on the floor (unless the coach has just varnished it). If it is in a room where there is no rake to the audience, you must put it on a platform.

Use folding stages or platforms put together to make a nice size playing area. (Your stage directions will still follow those that are listed for those "rich people" with stages.) You will have to spend extra rehearsal time practicing getting on and off the platforms with minimal bone breakage, but it is not impossible.

Set changes will have to be done in front of the audience. (Do not expect to throw the theatre into complete blackness and have some poor stage crew change George Washington's home to "A City In Brazil" in complete darkness! They have to see what they're doing!)

Also, your cast may have to be standing next to the platform, waiting to go on. You might want to consider this when building sets and build a couple of extra flats for either side of the stage to hide behind. (Mom and Dad will not watch the action on stage, no matter how riveting it is with little Sally standing on the side, waving like crazy, in her butterfly costume.)

The stage is no mystery, but make sure you understand it and its' complexities before you bring on the onslaught of kiddies, or the next stage you'll be looking forward to will be the one out of town.

Chapter 7

"WHERE DO I FIND A GIANT FOR 'JACK AND THE BEANSTALK' IN THIRD GRADE?"

(Finding The Cast)

You are now ready to begin. (And you thought we'd never make it this far......Ye of little faith!)

You have the scripts. You know your stage. You have your staff. Now all you need is the cast.

Let's talk about this for a moment.

Just who are you working with? Hmmmm? Will your cast be kids who are forced into this because their fourth period teacher wants to get rid of them? Will you be able to really cast the show or will parts be assigned by you or another leader? What ages will you be dealing with? Can they read? Can they talk? Will you be dealing with any disabled children? Hyperactive children? Are any of them overly sensitive to the sight of an adult putting her head down on a desk and muttering, "And I was voted most likely to succeed Marlo Thomas in high school?"

Take a look at your prospective cast. You may have to make some startling changes in your script, if you are confronted by all girls when you were planning "King Arthur", or a group of small children who have not mastered their "A-B-C's" when you wanted to do "King Lear". Try to find out what type of response the plays have gotten in the past. (That's right. Go visit your predecessor in the rest home. She should be able to have visitors by now.)

Learn to adapt to fit the cast. Perhaps your Giant in "Jack And The Beanstalk" is only four foot three. He can be a giant among lesser men! Or your "Goldilocks" lacks yellow hair. Who's going to notice besides the audience? And they'll go along with anything! After all, they are parents.

Be aware of the kids who are in wheelchairs or have sight disabilities. Of course you'll use them! Just make sure that you can assure their safety when getting up and down the stage. Do not limit yourself by looking for the perfect child to play "Sleeping Beauty". Remember, "beauty is in the eye of the beholder", and every child who tries out for your play is that!

GETTING THEM INTERESTED

If you are going to advertise for a cast, either throughout the school or on the playground or city wide, then you will have to put out an audition flyer telling the world you are looking for thirty-five kids to become "stars".

This is where your publicity chairperson will come in. They have sent a press release to the newspapers, hopefully, telling of your casting days. (See Chapter 15 on "Publicity".)

In most cases, you won't need talent as much as you will need bodies to fill the stage up. Start talking it up at the schools or playgrounds you work. Begin early dispelling the notion that acting is for sissies. Don't make the play "too cute" or the flyer advertising for a cast so precious that the football playing kids will choke on it......Or worse, make fun of it!

Treat it like an adult endeavor. Make it an exciting challenge and tell them what a fun time will be had by all those who attend. Try to downplay the competitive nature of casting and let them know in advance what to expect. (Once you've figured it out yourself.)

Make sure you not only tell the children what time casting begins, make sure their parents are aware what time it is over, lest you be stuck with several kiddies while mommy and daddy do their Saturday shopping.

Schedule the casting (and rehearsals) at a time when kids are available. If you are at a school, immediately after is a good time (along with soccer, baseball, ballet, etc., etc.). If at a park or community hall, find out what time schools let out and give them enough time to make it to the rehearsal hall.

Saturday mornings are OK, but make it late enough that if parents have to drive, they get to sleep-in at least a little!

Remember, you are in competition with every youth team in the city. Make being in a play a great event!

BEATING THE BUSHES......AGAIN!

What happens after you have done a media blitz and you still don't have enough kiddies?

Welcome to the world of children's theatre.

This is a natural. Go out and start beating those bushes. Go to local schools or other classrooms. Put up flyers in the library and any available space kids meet. Start recruiting by making sure everyone realizes what fun putting on a show is.

If this fails, try bribery. Perhaps let word leak out about the fantastic cast party you "always" have. Maybe someone finds out that if they are in the school play, they can get out of study period once a week or get a chance to have their picture in the paper. Find out what appeals to your potential actors and use it.

WORD OF WARNING: Do not lie to them.

If you are advertising freedom from homework once a week or photos in the newspaper or whatever.....make sure you can come across! Lie once and you will never get a kid to come back for another play. (That's a threat, not a promise.)

After all the bushes are beaten and there is still a lack of participants, you may realize the play you have chosen is wrong or that there is no interest in theatre at this time. In which case, you can use the children you have and either alter the play you chose ("Snow White And The Two Dwarfs") or do another play (which usually disappoints the kiddies who had their heart set on "Springtime Follies").

You can also go back to your production team and honestly tell them that before sinking any more money into the endeavor, they should realize there is not much interest in theatre now. Review your options and decide if you really want to expend so much time and energy to a production that has minimal interest at this time. It is better to cancel early on that wait until parents have rearranged schedules to get little Herbert to rehearsals only to find after three of them, the play has been cancelled.

ON THE OTHER HAND

What do you do if you get too many kids?

Sometimes, a really popular play pulls in a couple of hundred kids to audition. Hopefully, you will be doing a play with a lot of "merry villagers" who can clomp on stage, sing a song or two, and clomp off while the action continues.

If you won't be able to use all those who try out, try to encourage some of those with "less than desired talent" to help out backstage. (Making sure that they are responsible enough to actually help out.) It is sometimes a big boost to the morale of a kid who didn't get a part, or one who is the "third villager on the left" to be made "Prop Master" in charge of making sure Robin Hood's arrows are on stage left at the needed moment. Everyone likes to feel important. Make each cast member feel that way.

Chapter 8

"GET ME 'THE BRADY BUNCH' QUICKLY!"

(Auditions)

Remember "A Chorus Line" with the group of dancers who are desperately seeking a part ("I really need this job.....Oh God, I need this job.....")? Remember the drama and pathos as each one tried to outshine the others? Remember "The Brady Bunch" as they decide to put on a show and they all pop up with some wonderful talent that, up until that moment, had gone unnoticed? Remember good old Mickey and Judy who come from a town where every kid could play a musical instrument, tap dance, mime, juggle and paint sets?

Remember those great cinematic moments?

Wake up and welcome to the world of P.S. 54's school play and a good healthy dose of reality.

Your auditions will be eye-opening to you (that is, if you are given the luxury of casting your own show). The main point to remember is not to make them as taxing to the kids as "A Chorus Line". It should be fun. (You remember "fun", don't you? That's what Veronica Volunteer promised you you'd have directing this extravaganza.)

BEFORE "THEY" COME

You have advertised where and when auditions are and you have arrived early enough to make sure that the auditorium doors are unlocked (and given yourself enough time to hunt down the custodian to open the doors when you find they are not unlocked). You have arrived with enough copies of the script, the scenes you have decided to audition, and pencils and cards for your young actors and actresses.

Before they arrive, make sure the stage area is clear and you have enough lights to see them. Also, make sure you have enough chairs for them as well. You and your assistants (hopefully, they are on board by now) have decided who will be responsible when a kid starts getting bored or starts making rude noises (a favorite pastime while waiting to go on).

Set up a desk away from the stage and away from the potential actors where you will sit and "direct". Make sure the chair is comfortable because it is going to be a long day.

WHEN THEY COME

As the kiddies start to arrive for the audition, have your assistant standing at the door. As each parent tries to come in, have your assistant kindly but FIRMLY say, "I'm sorry, but no parents are allowed in during auditions. There is coffee and tea available next door and we will be finished at approximately 4 p.m. Thank you."

DO NOT LET PARENTS INTO THE AUDITION HALL. (Please reread this statement over, one hundred times!)

This is important! Kids clam up with parents watching and parents tend to react as if their kid is up for the part in a major motion picture.

I guarantee you will get a hundred excuses why a parent MUST be present while little Alice sings "Girls Just Wanna Have Fun" (for a "Pinochio" audition?). But be firm.

Say NO!

As the actors and actresses enter, have your assistant hand them a card like the one that follows. You may not need all the information, but having them fill it out will keep them busy for a few minutes until everyone has arrived.

If they cannot read or write yet, simply have someone fill out their name and phone number for them.

Keep them busy during those first few minutes. If they don't know each other, this may be the only quiet time you have with them.....ever again.

If you are doing a "classic", why not play some of the music from those Disney versions as they come in to set the mood? If you are doing an original, play some other music or have your musical director play a song or two from the show. Keep it light and fun.

SAMPLE AUDITION CARD

NAME:

PHONE:

ADDRESS:

HOMEROOM: (If a school play)

ANY OTHER PLAYS YOU HAVE DONE:

PART YOU WOULD LIKE TO TRY OUT FOR: (If doing classics)

GRADE POINT AVERAGE:

WHAT MUSICAL INSTRUMENT DO YOU PLAY?

DO YOU DANCE? IF SO, WHAT KIND?

HOW DO YOU SING? GOOD_____ NOT SO GOOD_____

WHAT OTHER SCHOOL OR OUTSIDE ACTIVITIES ARE YOU CURRENTLY ENROLL-ED IN?

YOU'RE ON!

At the appointed hour (or ten minutes after to allow anyone who is skateboarding over a few possible detours), begin by welcoming everyone and introducing yourself.....even if they are all from your own class. For some reason, being in a new situation, seeing you in "real clothes" instead of teaching clothes, kids forget who you are.

Explain the play to them and, if it is a classic, ask how many are familiar with it. If the group is small, go around and ask everyone their name and what stage experience they have had. Encourage those who have had none that this will be fun and that you are always looking for new talent. Tell those who have done other shows that this may be a new experience for them as well since no two plays are done the same way.

Ask how many do not read, even if you have advertised for a cast over the age of seven or eight. Sometimes, little kids come with big brothers and sisters and are anxious to be in the show as well. If they don't read, have them recite something so you can hear their voice. Small parts can be memorized with some drilling from mom or dad, so don't hesitate to use these "munchkins", if they have a loud voice.

Explain that loudness and clarity are important and the audience must hear them from "the house" (remember that word?).

Do not be alarmed if they stare at you blankly as you do this speech. After all, you are an adult and know precious little about anything. ("If you were so hot acting in high school, how come you don't know Don Johnson?")

Begin by asking who wants to play the lead characters. Do not cry when they all raise their hands. After all, what little girl really wants to play a "mean, ugly step sister" if the other option is "Cinderella"?

Remember this simple little rule.....MAKE ALL THE PARTICIPANTS FEEL LIKE STARS!

You will have one or two shy ones who are hesitant to raise their hands when asked if they want to play "The Fairy Princess". These are kids who have not left their self concept at the door. They see that there is a room full of blonde, perfect looking Fairy Princesses and have decided, in self defeat, to be satisfied playing the Chimney Sweep. DON'T LET THIS HAPPEN!

A Fairy Princess does not have to be blond and beautiful. Cinderella does not have to be the most popular kid in school. Tom Sawyer need not be the boy who is also captain of the football team!

Take risks. This is an opportunity for a child who has low self esteem to blossom. Make every person in your play feel as if they are the star. Even at auditions! (Am I on my soap box? Can you tell who was the tall, skinny kid in the back row of every production of his school play back in the late 'Fifties?)

Don't immediately leap upon the obvious choices at auditions. Keep it light and fun for EVERYONE!

READING FOR PARTS

Pick a short scene that has two or three people talking in equal parts. A page of dialogue should give you an idea of how they handle parts. Choose three potential stars and take their audition cards from them. Have them go to the playing area and read the scene, informing them to be loud and energetic. Try to choose a scene that has a minimum of difficult words! The audition will take forever as your potential King stumbles over such words as "the" and "for", not to mention staring in disbelief at words such as "proclaim" and "merriment".

Even top students become poor readers during the audition. There is something intimidating to children about reading a script since they are not used to the format.

Gently prod them with words they are unfamiliar with and tell them the parts in parenthesis are called stage directions and need not be read. (As in the case "Oh, Little Red Ridinghood moving stage right and taking the basket you are the most wonderful grandchild in the world kissing her on the head.")

Patiently explain that the wad of bubble gum lodged in the cheek detracts from the believability that little Billy is really a Lord Chamberlain and that if he would kindly deposit it in the trash, we could really accept this acne ridden preteen with the "Kowabunga" T-shirt as an English nobleman.

Give everyone a chance to read the same scene. It will get monotonous, I guarantee it. By the fortieth time you have corrected the word "Huzzah", you will be seriously considering quitting the endeavor.

As each child reads, check their audition card. Jot down notes to help you remember which kid is which (I know.....I know.....They all look alike to you!) A quick note of "Brown hair, glasses" or "Tall blonde" will help when you are sitting at home trying to remember which was the best Friar Tuck.

Try to come up with a rating guide that will help you decipher your own thoughts. Make it all positive in case one of the little darlings happens to look over your shoulder.

For example, as a child reads you might jot down any of the following:

"Very Good" - (Translation: The kid is a serious contender for the part.)

"Good Interpretation" - (Consider for a minor part.)

"Nice Job" - (Maybe he could pull the curtain.)

You may want to use a number code to help establish a ranking. In this case, use only high numbers. A kid who sees that you've written "104" on his card may think he's great, but you know you're only looking at the "4" on a scale of one to ten.

When everyone has read, you can recall the kids you want to see act together. This time, try putting potential lead material with other potential lead material. Have them read a new scene to see if they can handle new material.

Remember: This is not Broadway. Keep it light and fun. The whole process for an hour show with, say fifteen characters, should not take more than an hour and a half.

The kids will get bored just sitting there so divide them up, if possible, with your assistant taking some outside to get rid of "excess energy".

If your show is going to have music, have the musical director teach the kids a song and listen to their voices as they sing.

If your show is going to have a lot of movement, (notice I didn't say "dancing"!) put on a record and let them "boogie" to see those who really can handle the few basic steps you've devised.

At the end of your audition, have all the kids get on stage, tallest to shortest from stage left to stage right. This will let you get an idea of who can play "parents" (usually the taller kids) or what coupling looks good together. DO NOT CAST JUST BY PHYSICAL QUALITIES! There is not one law that says Rumplestiltskin has to be the shortest. But this will give you an idea of the different levels you will be working with.

Thank everyone for attending. Let them know then how you will notify the cast of the parts. For some, putting a cast list in the window of the school hall the next day relieves the face to face confrontation that although they read beautifully, you decided to cast someone else in their "role of a lifetime".

Other directors will phone the child he has cast or send a letter. Brave ones will announce the cast right there at the auditions. (Maybe you can sleep with the memory of a five year old staring at you in disbelief that she didn't get the part.)

However you decide to let your cast know, tell the children then. They are anxious and want to know the results immediately. Do not drag this on for two or three weeks, making up your mind. They will lose interest. They should be notified within one or two days.

Also, tell them the rehearsal schedule and remind them that this is a commitment. Make sure there are no secret vacation plans around the corner that will have your cast romping at the beach and not on the stage.

Tell them how impressed you are at the talent before you and let them know if you will be using all those who auditioned or only a select few. Impress on them how difficult your decision will be due to the tremendous pool of talent and thank them again for their participation.

Open the doors and return the little darlings to their parents, who undoubtedly have been sitting with their ears to the door the entire hour and a half.

CHOOSING THE CAST

You are now alone with all those little cards that have childlike scrawls on them. It is up to YOU to pick the best darn Ebeneezer Scrooge this town has ever seen.

This is when it is nice to have an assistant who has been with you throughout the audition process. While you stand, holding a child's card, screaming, "Who is Janie Jones?", your assistant, hopefully, will pipe up with, "The little red headed girl with glasses. She was good, remember?" It really helps to have another pair of eyes there.

Your assistant should also be able to help you by indicating how well the child in question interacted with the others while outside. (I doubt that a casting director ever wonders if Paul Newman and Robert Redford can "play well together" as a casting requirement, but then, you're not in Hollywood!)

Stack the cards into the parts you think each kid is best suited for and then go back and whittle down the stack until you have found the right star. Sometimes you will have an over abundance of talent for one role while there is no one who can really handle another part. Be flexible.

When casting, try to vary the leads from one production to another. Just because Harvey was a great "Petunia" in your "Ode To Spring", doesn't mean he will be a terrific "Father Christmas" in December's production.

Every town has its prima donnas and I find that giving the lead to the same kid each time makes others not want to audition. Go with the underdog sometimes. Use this as a growing experience and let a plainer "Cinderella" do the job. (She will bloom before your eyes, I promise!) Make everyone a star for a little bit in their lives. I also know the underdog usually works harder than the seventh grader who has had everything handed to her.

As you make up your cast list, including hundreds of "merry villagers", also keep in the back of your mind the fact that sometimes kids drop out. Have an alternate planned for that very reason. Do not post the alternate list or announce it to anyone.....Just keep it in mind.

Many directors love to double cast. (Two kids get the same part and alternate playing it on different evenings.) They reason that this gives more kids an opportunity to "star" in the production.

I hate it.

There is always a competition that is not entirely healthy. Favoritism runs rampant and kids feel a bit lost without the continuity of familiar faces. If you have too many interested participant (from my typewriter keys to God's ears), think of doing TWO one act plays! Two casts means double the rehearsal time and often one group is short changed. But.....

Some directors use understudies so kids with smaller parts will feel important. Don't list your understudies unless you are willing to work with them. Giving a kid an understudy part does little for his ego, if the child is never allowed to rehearse or go on. Additionally, understudies really rarely are used in children's productions because the child who is understudying figures he won't go on and never learns the material. The director usually promises to work with the actor, but never gets around to it and understudies are expected to watch the other children do it and pick up through osmosis or some other clairvoyant trick.

Of course, following this advise will surely find you minus a Dorothy on the night "Oz" opens, but if that's the case, **you** can always go on.

Be creative in your casting. I've already discussed sexism. You will find more girls than boys trying out, so don't be afraid to use them in formerly "male dominated" roles. Just don't make them play men. It always strikes me odd seeing two little girls go off to live happily ever after, even though one has a fake beard. You can change certain characters (a page, a king to a queen, a wizard, etc.) to women. And if you search hard enough you will find a boy to play a prince.....although you may have to promise him that he won't have to wear tights.

RESEARCH YOUR STARS

If you are casting from a school pool of actors or a classroom situation where other teachers may know of the strength of weakness of some children, don't hesitate to corner the teacher and ask them their opinion. Simply say that you are considering little Susie for a role in the play. If she gasps and rolls her eyes, you may want to reconsider.

Find out if the potential star has a history of dropping out or is considered unruly by teachers. Also, be aware of commitments. If a child is playing soccer, running for class treasurer, is homeroom monitor and in charge of milk collection, he or she may be overextended.

Take into consideration the child's grade point average. Will taking on the addition of a play limit the child's study time? A kid whose grades start to slip will be yanked out of the school play by the parents. (Rightfully so, I begrudgingly add.) Ask his teachers if the additional load of the play will not make his grades suffer. (Better to find out now than a week before opening when mid-term grades are handed out.)

But once again, do not sweat the small stuff! After all your hours of analyzing and research, no matter who you cast, your best friend will avoid you in the super market (even though you swear their little darling is indeed talented but not ready to play "Lady Macbeth"), children will hate you and your assistant will finally throw up his hands and exclaim, "If you want to cast that little brat who kicked me as the King, go ahead.....It's your show!"

Don't worry. On opening night, these people will flock back to you to congratulate you on your remarkable insight and instincts in directing the play.

If not, you could always write a book.

Chapter 9

"WHAT DO YOU MEAN THE ONLY TIME I CAN SCHEDULE REHEARSALS IN THE GYM IS MIDNIGHT?"

(Scheduling)

Play Schedule...

SUNDAY 1	MONDAY 2	TUESDAY 3	WEDNESDAY 4	THURSDAY 5	FRIDAY 6	SATURDAY 7
	AUDITIONS 3:30pm		CAST PICKED	1st. rehearsal		
8	9 rehearsal	10	11 rehearsal	12	13 rehearsal	14 PRESS RELEASE TO PAPERS!
15	16 rehearsal	17	18 rehearsal	19 Set Done!	20 rehearsal	21 rehearsal
22	23 rehearsal	24 Costumes finished rehearsal	25 rehearsal	26 rehearsal	27 DRESS REHEARSAL!	28 OPENING NIGHT!!!
29	30					

things to do:

Between the time you cast the play and Opening Night, you are going to be stuck with this group of kiddies for several hours a day. This is the rehearsal process and is rarely shown in those old movies of "putting on a show". They never really let you see a director trying to get a star out of a locked bathroom or trying to solve the puzzle of who pinched who first or climbing up a tree to retrieve a script someone has tossed up there.

That's Entertainment!

Before you first rehearsal, there are a few more things to check.

YOUR THEATRE

Remember to book your rehearsal hall. Be mindful that a multipurpose room is just that.....multi purpose! Do you know what class is using the room before you? Is it an aerobic class that will leave the room smelling like an old gym sock or a youth band that will leave you with a stage filled with music stands that refuse to be folded?

Do not expect complete use of the room since you "are doing theatah!". You will have to beg, borrow and steal as many minutes as you can before the girl's volleyball team runs in, destroying your quaint village set.

Make sure you have the correct keys to the facilities.....(Does this tell you that I have been locked out before?)

Have your set designed so you can start moving your actors around. Know how big everything is so you can warn the children of high steps, low ceilings, etc.

Have your scripts typed, collated and ready to hand out. If you are using rented scripts from a company, keep a master list and number each script.

Know your liabilities. How responsible for these kids are you? Have they signed releases in case they are injured? Are they covered by the parks' or schools' insurance?

Ban parents from the rehearsal hall. This will keep your sanity and let the parents fully enjoy the show on opening night. Thank them for bringing their children and calmly, but firmly tell them to take a hike.

Be sure you have numbers to call when the parent is late coming to pick up the child or a place that you can leave the child supervised until the parent returns.

Have all your handouts typed, duplicated and ready to be.....well,.....handed out. If you are working with a large group of "unknown" kiddies, you may consider having name tags for them. They could include their real names and their character names.

REHEARSAL SCHEDULES

Most importantly.....Have your rehearsal schedule finished.

This sounds like a lot of work and, surprise, it is! But it is worth it. You should have your entire rehearsal time mapped out and know exactly what you are going to do at each one. (This is not set in concrete, of course, but you can't help impress people when, on the first day of rehearsal, you hand out a plan of attack.....Even if you have no intention of really sticking to it.)

Your rehearsal schedule will not only be of help to you, but to your cast and crew as well.

It should include times of rehearsal, what will be done at the rehearsals, deadlines for crew assignments, location of rehearsals and any information that anyone at any-time would have the remotest desire to know.....Now, isn't that simple?

Don't panic. It is not that difficult once you begin to logically think through what you want and when you want it. ("Yesterday", is not a correct answer.)

Start by thinking how long you want to rehearse and the number of rehearsals you will need to put together this extravaganza.

Meeting every day after school for one hour, you can do a twenty minute to thirty minute play in three to four weeks. However, this is a strain on your crew to put together a full set and costumes so I would stretch it to five weeks, if possible. (If this is your first time out, don't hesitate to stretch it to six or seven weeks and use the filler rehearsal time with games and activities.)

Longer plays of an hour or more may involve six to seven weeks rehearsing daily for an hour.

Don't make your rehearsals more than an hour and a half, if you are going daily. If you will meet only once a week (Saturday mornings, usually), you can go to a couple of hours and stretch the period over ten weeks, but be warned, kids get bored easily.....I get bored easily, too, and the idea of ten weeks is a bit much!

You may want to start a staggered rehearsal schedule, meeting on Monday, Wednesday, and Friday for the first few weeks and then switch over to a full week the last few weeks of rehearsal.

Whatever you choose, be consistent. Don't say, "We'll only rehearse on Fridays and Saturdays", and then call five weeks of "special" Monday and Tuesday rehearsals.

Being consistent with starting and ending times also helps car pools from sinking. Parents will have to adjust their schedules as well as the little kiddies, so be considerate. Would YOU want to sit in a cold car on a rainy day while you get in "just one more hour" of practice?

I don't like to stagger the times the kids are due either. (That is, King and Queen come at 3:30, Prince at 4:00 and Cinderella at 4:30.) This too, drives car pools crazy, especially if you have brothers and sisters in the same play. Either they will all come together anyway, or you will get great excuses like, "They were retarring Maple Street and I wanted to watch.", when your Prince strolls in late. Make it easy to remember that their tiny souls belong to you from X until Y daily until further notice.

Once you have slaved and worked on your rehearsal schedule, you will have to revamp it time and time again. Don't worry. Just notify your young actors AND THEIR PARENTS as soon as you learn your rehearsal hall is flooded, that your root canal just won't wait, that your lead has the chicken pox and has just exposed the entire cast, that there is a new special school schedule letting the kids out at noon on your day of a three o'clock rehearsal or any other small catastrophe that may waltz your way.

Following is a sample rehearsal schedule. Notice that it allows the cast to know Where, When, and What will be rehearsed. It shows the crew their deadlines and shows, and whenever possible, changes in the normal rehearsal schedule.

I send this home at the first rehearsal. I also send it with the attached letter to parents. This will help clue me into vacation plans, doctor appointments and any other KNOWN valid excuse for a missed rehearsal.

REHEARSAL SCHEDULE

Date	Time	Place	Who Attends?	Additional Information
May 4	3-4 p.m.	Recreation Hall	All Cast	
May 5	3-4 p.m.	Recreation Hall	All Cast	Costume Measurements Taken
May 6	3-4 p.m.	Recreation Hall	All Cast	
May 7	3-4 p.m. 3-4 p.m. 4-5 p.m.	Recreation Hall Room 14 Room 14	Dancers Mushrooms Beansprouts	
May 8	3-4 p.m.	Veterans Hall (This rehearsal only)	All Cast	
May 10	3-4 p.m.	Recreation Hall	All Cast	Publicity Photos taken Lead costumes needed
May 11	5-7 p.m. (NOTE TIME)	Recreation Hall LINES MEMORIZED BY NOW	All Cast	Lighting crew to check lights
May 12	NO REHEARSAL	NO REHEARSAL	NO REHEARSAL	Crew Head Meeting 7 p.m. at Recreation Hall
May 13	3-4 p.m.	Recreation Hall	Merry Villagers	Program Information due
May 16	3-4 p.m.	Recreation Hall	All Cast	
May 17	3-4 p.m.	Room 14	The Monsters	Costume fittings for Monsters only
May 18	3-4 p.m.	Room 14	The Monsters	Press Releases out
May 19	3-4 p.m.	Recreation Hall	All Cast	Makeup crew meeting 4:30 p.m. at Rec Hall
May 20	3-6 p.m. (NOTE LONGER HOURS: BRING A SNACK)	Recreation Hall	DRESS REHEARSAL	Makeup crew/costumes sets due
May 21	3-6 p.m.	Recreation Hall	Final Dress	Makeup crew arrives 2:30 p.m. Stage crew arrives 4:30 p.m. Sets finished

SAMPLE LETTER TO PARENTS

Dear Parent:

Your child has been cast in the upcoming St. James School production of "A Streetcar Named Leon". Attached, please find a copy of our rehearsal schedule. Review the schedule and see if any dates conflict with upcoming vacations, doctor appointments or other family activities and make a note of this at the bottom of this page. In case of an emergency or an illness, please call the front office at 555-3452 ext 54 and let them know your child will miss rehearsals.

Please note the ending time of the rehearsals. Be prompt in picking up your child.

Additionally, there are still some openings on our backstage crew. We need your help! Please? Thanks for your help. See you opening night!
- -

RETURN THIS PORTION AT THE NEXT REHEARSAL

My child_____ has my permission to participate in the school play. I have reviewed the rehearsal schedule and at present, he/she:

(CHECK ONE)

_____Will not miss any rehearsals

_____Will miss the following rehearsal dates:

_____

Signed:_____

You may want to keep your crew schedule on a separate sheet, but I find that parents put these on the refrigerator and sometimes it spurs them on to get involved also.

This is no means complete. I have compressed it somewhat so don't just run out and duplicate this. You have to make up one that fits your schedule the best.

DEADLINES

Your crew schedule should run parallel with your acting schedule. Your crew should be notified from the very first meeting when you expect something from them. For example:

SETS   Should be due two weeks before the show. Lots of luck with that. Don't be alarmed when they are only there for the last dress rehearsal.....and still unpainted. But just the same, demand they be ready two weeks before just to keep up your image and relax, knowing you've given yourself a fat cushion to fall back on.

COSTUMES   Try for one week before the show in case there are fitting problems. Have them completed by then, but don't use them all together until dress rehearsal or you'll end up with a Christopher Columbus with torn tights.

PROPS   As props become available, use them.....UNLESS THEY ARE FRAGILE OR RENTED. Try to have them all at least a week before the show.

PHOTOS   For publicity.....Have these done immediately after casting during the first or second week of rehearsal.

PRESS
RELEASE   To the newspapers AT LEAST two weeks prior to the show. Give yourself time to have it approved by officials and check spelling with cast.

I like to sit down with a huge calendar and colored marking pens and plot out the entire schedule, using different colors for each crew. (Green for props, Blue for sets, etc.) There is no reason for this except it keeps my mind occupied for a few hours and the different colors look nice while I am drawing lines through due dates, changing rehearsal locations and cancelling photos.

As you plan your rehearsal schedule, just remember the three "B's":

Be creative

Be Adaptable

Be sure your health insurance covers mental duress.

Chapter 10

STEPHEN SPEILBERG AND ME

(Directing Tips)

THE FIRST DAY

The enemy approaches. You can smell them coming down the hall, their presence preceded by the scent of uneaten lunches of peanut butter sandwiches. You can hear their tiny voices reaching decibels way above the approved noise control. (And these are the children to who you will soon be yelling, "I can't hear you beyond the first row!?") They're coming and you are ready!

That's right.

You are ready for them. You've done your homework. You've done your duplicating. You have all the forms you need, the scripts you need, the staff you need. Now all you have to do is direct the darn thing.

Relax. You have that under control too.

As the kiddies come in, have them set down again and welcome each one by name, if you can remember it. Start by introducing yourself again and your assistants as well. Welcome them and tell them how happy you are that you are going to be in this play together.

Hand out your rehearsal schedule and the letter to the parents, insisting that the letter with permission be returned by the next rehearsal.

RULES

Start by reciting the rules that you expect everyone to follow. (They will stare at you wide eyed, thinking, "Rules? I thought this would be fun!")

Make it fun, but make sure they realize there is more to putting on a play than jumping on the stage and dancing around.

Some of my rules that I usually try to get across are:

1) No gum at rehearsal.....Even if you have a non speaking role.

2) Do not jump off the stage onto the auditorium floor. If the fall doesn't break your legs, I may.

3) Do not touch the curtains.

4) Do not touch the props that don't belong to you.

5) Do not touch the scenery.

6) Do not touch the director while he/she is crying.

7) No running in the auditorium. (This is always broken, but give it a shot!)

8) Three inexcusable missed rehearsals and you will be replaced. (It's a good threat and usually scares them into calling you before a missed rehearsal.)

9) There are no "stars" in this play. We all pull our own weight.

After you finish this speech, hand out the scripts. If you are renting the scripts or need to have them back, tell the kiddies how much their parents can be expected to shell out if they lose it down the manhole on Fifth Street on their way to rehearsal.

On rented material, you may want to put a number on each one and keep a list with which kid has what script, so when it comes time to hand them back, you will know.

Hopefully, you have given them scripts to keep (something kids love to have) and to lose (something kids love to do).

If the scripts are theirs to keep, I have them write their names on the front and back in big crayons so it can be spotted sitting in the auditorium from the stage. If they are a young group, I have them draw their character on it as well, to really personalize it.

BLOCKING

After all this "boring stuff", get down to business right away. Don't have them read through the script. Get them up on their feet and start to block the first scene. ("Blocking" is the stage movements their illustrious director.....you.....will give them.)

Divide the group up and start with the first scene. Have those who are involved in that scene go up on the stage. Have the others go with your costumer to be measured or with your assistant to start some theatrical games.

Take the group you have and explain that you will tell them when and where to move. They should WRITE THIS MOVEMENT DOWN IN PENCIL IN THEIR SCRIPT next to the line they move on. (Keep a bunch of pencils with erasers handy.)

Disregard the blocking that is already in the script. ("Lester turns R. and walks UC, laughing. He goes off UL, dropping a rose DL.") That may have worked on Broadway or in the theatre where the author wrote it, but it may not work for you.....especially if you aren't certain what a UC is. Explain that to the kiddies as well. The only blocking you want them to follow is the one you give to them. (Of course, use those stage directions as guidelines!)

Your script should have all the blocking down prior to rehearsal. You have done your homework and know which side of the stage you will have your entrances and exits and when you want someone to "cross the stage in thought".

Your script should look like the following BEFORE you start rehearsal.

U.R.

(JANET and BILLY ENTER and see the SPIRIT OF SAFETY)   *X J.B.*

JANET

Oh, Billy, I'm frightened. *(PUT FLOWER DOWN)*

BILLY *STUTTERING*

What's.....So.....Soo.....scary? (He crosses to the SPIRIT) Please, Mr. Spirit, could

you help us?

SPIRIT

~~Come, Children.~~ *CUT* *KINDLY* Tell me what you want.   *JANET FOLLOWS BILLY*

BILLY

We've lost our way and need to get home.   *X DR*   *TURN TO THEM*

SPIRIT

You've lost your way? How odd. I have heard of losing many things, but not a way.

I will show you the road home. (THEY EXIT as KING LEONARDO SNEAKS IN)

U.R.   *D.L.*

Those are not hieroglyphics all over the page. Those are the director's notes made prior to rehearsal and ALWAYS IN PENCIL. You have written in where all entrances and exits will be made (using abbreviations such as U.C. for "Up Center", etc.), you have drawn little diagrams to show where the movement occurs, you have added any "characterization" you want (such as, "stuttering", or "thoughtfully") in order to tell the actor, and you have made deletions and additions to dialogue and action when you felt it was needed.

It only looks difficult, honest.

All you have to do is sit down and think of how you want your characters to move and jot it down. It should be a guideline for you much like a coach's playbook in sports. You can change it as you go, but at least if anyone grabs your script by mistake, you'll look like you know what's going on.

After a few rehearsals, when the kiddies have their blocking down, you won't even be looking at the script, but watching them instead.

As you do rehearsal and if you make changes in your blocking, change it in your script. (Better yet, have your assistant change it, if possible.) You might want to show the young actors and actresses how you mark your script so they won't be afraid to write down blocking marks in their's.

If the kids are too young to write in their books, have another actor help them re-member. It is best when working with those small munchkins to keep movement at a minimum. Parents will "ooh" and "aah" these kiddies for just standing there.

However, there is no reason not to have movement with the older children. Even if the Spirit Of Spring is explaining the miracle of nature to Billy and Susie (who fell through the rabbit hole to find out what happened to Easter), they can move around. As the Spirit begins his story, he can walk away, "deep in thought". Billy and Susie can follow him "intrigued". They can all run behind the mushroom "frightened" at the noise they hear.

This is called motivation. It is why an actor moves on the stage. No one stands stock still in real life and your actors shouldn't either. Think of interesting ways to get them to move about the stage. MOTIVATE them.

HOW TO SUCCEED IN DIRECTING BY REALLY, REALLY TRYING!
(Some helpful hints for the novice and not-so novice director.)

1)   Don't bunch the kids up on stage during group scenes. Even the merry villagers have parents who want to see their little child third from the left in the back row. Spread them out.

2)   Don't have the kids just line up, however. ("But didn't he just say.....?") Have different groupings so the actors can be seen, but it doesn't look like a police line up.

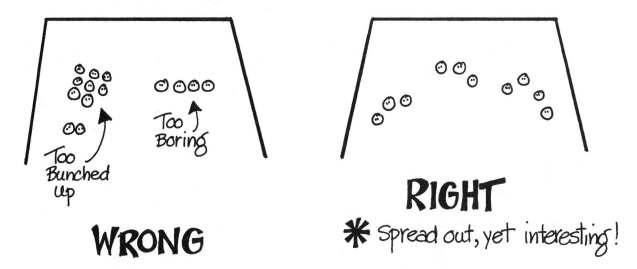

3)   Have the actors move AFTER they have said a line, not during. This ensures the audience has a running chance to hear the line unaccompanied by the sound of a sneaker squeaking across the floor.

4)   When a group is on stage, explain that scratching their knees, picking their noses or waving to audience members tend to lessen the believeability that they are in Fourteenth Century China. This is called "upstaging".....It means that while the detective is about to reveal the murderer, the corpse should not sneeze or any other member on stage should not move around "upstaging" the important action or dialogue on the stage. Teach them to stand still, but remain in character, if they are not talking.

5)   Have them listen to what's going on. Tell them to imagine that they never heard what is being said ever before, even though they have suffered through "thousands" of rehearsals. Acting is believing and reacting to what is going on around them while on stage.

6)   Once you have the kids "blocking down", don't change it without telling them. Make sure that they understand you are changing YOUR mind about blocking that doesn't work and that **they** didn't make a mistake. "But

last time I did it this way", is what they always say. Tell them, "Yes, and you did it well, but I am changing it now."

7) Try to cover a few pages a day. You do not have to do an entire scene to the end. Once you have done two or three pages of blocking, do it over again so they will have an understanding. Don't worry that you can't hear them as they will have their heads buried in their scripts. Right now, have them concentrate on getting familiar with the stage and moving on the right cue. Have them do each piece of blocking three times to get used to it.

8) Once you have done the first scene, move onto another one that will allow a few different actors on stage. Let them all get a chance during those first rehearsals to be "on stage".

9) Give them breaks. Lots of them. Even at an hour rehearsal, break it up so they can have ten minutes to run around the building and get some water.....a favorite pastime.

10) Be aware of where everyone is at all times. Do not become so engrossed in what is happening on stage that you are not aware of the group of kiddies who are experimenting as to whether the script is flushable or not.

KEEP IT FUN

As you block them, keep telling them over and over how important it is that they learn their lines and their blocking. If you go over the blocking three times, hopefully some of the lines will start to sink in. However, tell them to have parents quiz them on the lines during the times there are no rehearsals.

There are a million books out there on developing characterization and motivation, but your primary goal as a director of a school or camp pageant is to make sure your little darlings know their lines and can be heard. Move around the auditorium and see if the actors are visible and audible from all angles. If not, tell them to speak up or move their blocking so they can be seen.

At the end of the first rehearsal, remind them to return the letters of permission and to practice what you've done. Let them out at the appointed hour, even if it is in the middle of a scene.

At subsequent rehearsals, go over the scene you block last time and then start in on the new material. Set up a time when all the lines will have to be memorized (usually the middle part of rehearsals) and warn them to have those lines down or "woe unto them".

At each rehearsal, they will become more and more comfortable with the stage, with you, with each other. Keep it light, but always tell them how important it is they speak up.

As props, sets and costumes start popping up, include them, if you can, into the rehearsal setting. The more the kids know what something will look like, the less likely they are that they will break it during a show.

Use your assistants and musical director and other "hanger-oners" to keep the kids busy with other activities. Have them paint sets, design programs, cut out flowers, etc. (We always used a lot of flowers on stage. It gave the small parters something to do and made the stage look very festive.)

Try to keep the activities theatre oriented. Play theatre games or simply go over the lines when not on stage. You will also be amazed, as you rehearse, that many of the children enjoy watching the play when they are not on the stage. You can keep one eye on them as you direct and check out their reactions. Even after seeing it fifteen times, if they still laugh at the right places, you're doing OK.

BUMS KNOW!

Be open to suggestions. Once while directing a teenage play in the park, we were stumped as to how to have John Smith brought before the Indian Council with his hands tied. If the Indians pushed him down, the actor would fall on his face since his hands were bound behind him. I didn't want to lose the image of the settler being tied up, but didn't want to risk hurting my young actor. A bum in the park who had come to every rehearsal and watched from a distance, walked up and, reeking of cheap wine, said, "Why don't you tie his hands in **front** of him.....That way he could break his fall." The suggestion worked and the bum was given a couple of free tickets to opening night. It just shows you that good suggestions can come from almost any-where.

Listen to the bums!

Chapter 11

"I CAN'T FIND THE LADYBUG COSTUME IN A SIZE 3"

(Costumes)

Edith Head would stab me with her pins if she found out, but my entire philosophy of costumes can be summed up with, "If it fits, you wear it!" Many of the costumes I have used in shows have been found in garage sales or cut down from mom and dad's old clothes. You will be amazed at what you can find at junk stores, if you look.

But **you** shouldn't be looking. You should have a costume person coordinating all this.

Costumes do more than keep your third grade class play from being raided for immodesty. Costumes set a time and mood. They can identify a character right away. (Give the good guy a white hat!) They will tell the audience if a character is rich, poor, old, young and many other details that would require pages of dialogue. But most importantly, costumes allow the kiddies to look cute when mom and dad are snapping their photos to mail to grannie and grandpa.

You will be forgiven scenery falling, kids forgetting entrances, lines being mumbled and an auditorium whose air conditioning has quit, if the the kids look good. Get a costumer who understands your limits and is excited about the play. A parent or interested older brother and sister is a good bet. Try the community colleges for students majoring in theatre arts. (They might even have access to the college's drama department's wardrobe! See how sneaky you've become?)

The costumer should come to a lot of rehearsals since kids:

A)   Grow fast.

B)   Drop out, leaving you to replace the six foot giant with a three foot kid.

C)   Like to see their costumes.

D)   Can actually help with some of the easier work. (Like gluing on parts of their costumes.)

The costumer has the actors measurements from the first rehearsal (since, as a good director, you have allotted time for her to take these). She should also have her budget and her time schedule with enough time to correct any errors that may have been made.

BUDGET YOUR COSTUMES

A simple show with fifteen characters can go over a couple of hundred dollars in costumes alone. Let your costumer know that the Blue Fairy in "Pinocchio" does not have to appear in yards and yards of silk and gossamer. Cotton material is fine.

Costumes should be inexpensive, but should never look cheap to the kids. Chances are, your sets are going to be less than Broadway, so the costumes should give each child a feeling of being special. Never budget fifty dollars for the lead's costume and tell a minor character, "Oh, we'll get you something". Every costume should be treated as if it cost a fortune.

Many children's theatre companies keep their costumes in storage, so check out local schools and camps and see how good your bartering skills are. Sometimes local groups will rent out their outfits. Make sure you have allotted this cost (and the cost of dry cleaning the costumes before returning) in your budget.

Inform your costumer when you need the costumes and, after picking her up off the floor, see if you can get mothers and fathers to help.

When parents are asked to help, they should be given a bolt of cloth, a pattern and definite instructions. Do not let your costumer be vague and tell them, "Oh, just make a simple dirndl". Veronica Volunteer will spend a bloody fortune at an exclusive dressmaker to have her child's dirndl look as if it was ordered from Neiman Marcus. Be exacting as to what trims, colors, etc., your costumer wants.

Do not expect all parents to supply a costume. This is really not fair. Many parents are not sewing these days or are not crazy about rummaging around a swap meet looking for a Victorian stove pipe hat. I don't think asking kids to bring the necessities is bad. Socks, shorts, shirts, ties are all things that can usually be pulled from a kid's wardrobe. A complete Thumper The Bunny costume, I find, very few kids own.

Have your costumer do a few sketches of how elaborate the costumes are going to be. Remember, you both should know the script. If a magician is supposed to pull flowers from his sleeve, it pays to have the costumer aware of this and make the sleeves long.

Be creative with your costumes. Cinderella doesn't have to have a special dress that looks "just like the picture in this book". Use her mother's old formal! A prince can look princely in a cape and a pair of levis!

A FEW "QUICKIE" COSTUMES

Here are some low cost suggestions for costumes.

THE MULTI PURPOSE TUNIC

This is such an easy costume that I have used it over and over again in variations and no parents have ever been any the wiser.

Take a couple of yards of material, solid colored, cut a hole about ten inches in diameter right in the center and slip it over your young actor's head. Voila!

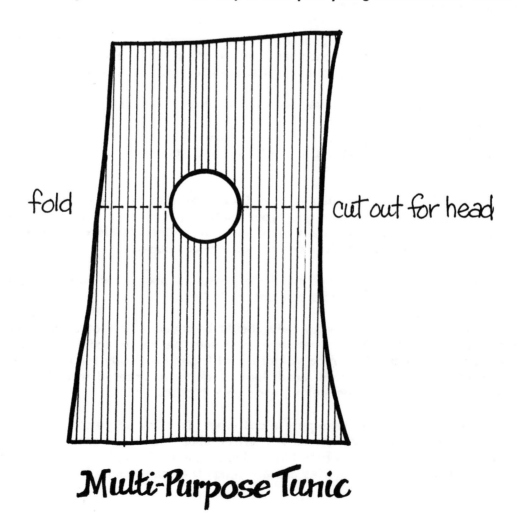

fold ----- cut out for head

Multi-Purpose Tunic

You now have a tunic fit for a prince (add a cape), a blouse for a peasant (have a long sleeved shirt underneath and add a belt).

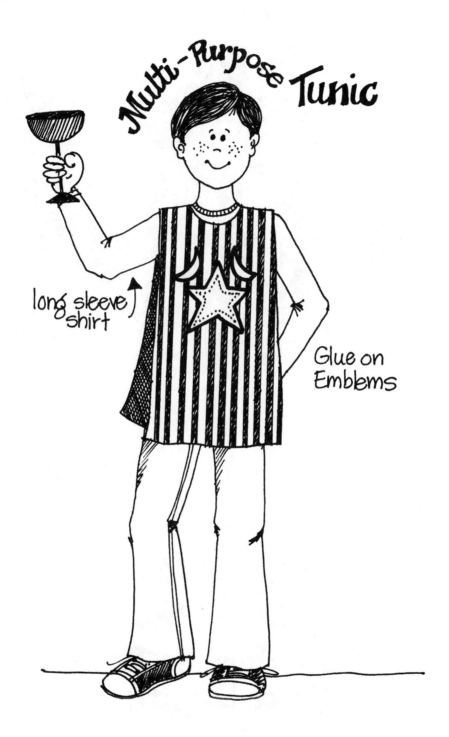

Or, by making it floor length, a gown for a magician or sorcerer.

long-sleeve shirt

Add sash and felt decorations

floor length Tunic

Multi-Purpose Tunic
(Floor Length)

Hem the ends, if you wish, and have the kids glue on felt designs to make it "personalized". It even makes blue jeans look regal! In a pinch, you can use crepe paper!

KNIGHT

Take a burlap bag that potatoes come in (you may have to visit a produce market for this) and spray paint it silver. Cut a neck hole and two arm holes and suddenly you have a "graile". Put it over grey sweat pants and your knight is ready to do battle.

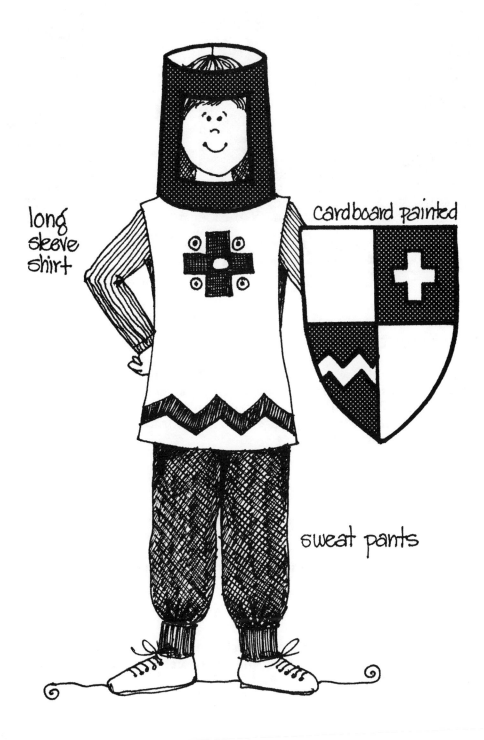

long sleeve shirt

cardboard painted

sweat pants

For a helmet, use a large piece of construction paper (blue or grey) and cut out a rectangle in the middle. Wrap it around, secure with tape and decorate with emblems. Slip it over your crusader's head and search for a dragon!

Knight's Helmet

ANIMAL COSTUMES

The parents still want to see their child even if he or she is playing a skunk. Make the basic costume out of pajama patterns and add a cap with ears sewn on. Don't make a full mask. Makeup can make Johnny look animalistic (although you may think he already does) and lets Mr. and Mrs. Johnny know that it is indeed their son up there.

BALL GOWNS

What mother has not been in a wedding and invested in a bridesmaid dress that hangs unworn but once in her closet? Use these and cut them down to size. Or go to the local thrift shop and pick one up for a couple of dollars. Hem it up using those iron-on hems in case mom wants her dress back.

TIGHTS

Boys hate them. I hate them. Most girls hate them. Let them wear long pants instead. Or sweat pants, now that they come in a variety of colors, make a good alternative.

CAPES

In a pinch, an old black **skirt** pinned to a collar makes a great cape.

CROWNS

Get some sturdy cardboard, cut out a crown and paint it gold. Use some old "precious" jewels from the thrift store and decorate. Use tons of glitter.

Of course, many things will have to be made.....Red Riding hoods, Peter Pan outfits, etc. Your costumer should coordinate all this. Make sure the costumer is aware of the colors of the set and the curtains used. Who could forget the hours of work that went into making Snow White's costume (an exact replica of the Disney version), all in gold velour only to find out on opening night that standing before the gold velour curtain, she disappeared? A stage full of red clad villagers standing behind the lead characters also dressed in red tends to make everyone look alike.

You may get a good deal on buying one color of material, but remember, you want the kids to stand out. Sometimes a bargain really isn't!

CARE OF COSTUMES

The day the final costumes arrive (hopefully, in plenty of time for alterations), take the cast aside and gently remind them of theatre etiquette. Tell them that the costumer has worked hard on their outfits and it really isn't the nicest thing to look at them and say, "Gross out!" Also, make it a rule that they are not to laugh at each other in costume. This tends to inhibit some of your stars as well.

However, your number one rule is never, NEVER, **NEVER** run while wearing costumes. This is a terrific way for a costume to meet with a puddle of mud outside or to get ripped on the banister of the stairs.

After you have had the costumer distribute the costumes, make arrangements for privacy for when they are trying the costumes on. Boys are reluctant to peel off their shirts in front of a group so make sure there are bathrooms for fittings, etc. Try not to have coed dressing rooms.

Your costumer may want a staff of her own to help distribute the costumes and, more importantly, collect them back. Have each child's name taped to a hanger so after dress rehearsals, they each go back on the rack in the right place.

DO NOT LET THE KIDDIES TAKE THEIR COSTUMES HOME! Even if Grandma is there only for the weekend and wants to see the costume, do not let them! This is a great opportunity to have the costumes disappear. (No, I am not accusing Grandma of hijacking your show!) After the cast has tried on the costumes, the costumer should have enough time to make the necessary alterations before the dress rehearsal. Keep all the costumes together.

Keep the costumes locked up between rehearsals. Crowns and magic wands are big temptations to little hands.

Tell your young thespians that if they leave a costume or a piece of their costume around, you might just take it and that kid will find himself on opening night in "The Emperor's New Clothes" even though the rest of the cast is doing "The Wind In The

Willows". (You may have to explain this to some of the younger ones, but the older kids should be able to pick up on your sarcasm.)

Keep a list of borrowed costumes and return them promptly after the show. Always have them dry-cleaned before returning.

Don't promise the kids costumes right out of a Flo Zigfield extravaganza and then give them construction paper. Be realistic with your ideas.

Try to get a couple of dress rehearsals in before the actual performance. The kids need to get used to wearing something besides their tennis shoes and "Go-Bot" T-shirts. I have seen many a show where Jack is too busy studying his hem than killing the giant. They will play with anything on the costume they haven't seen before.

Try your best to make each actor feel his or her costume is the most beautiful in the world.....Even the wicked witch's. With a little imagination, some money and a talented seamstress, the kids will be ready for all those photos mom and dad will take.

Chapter 12

"THE JOYS OF SETS"

(Designing Your Sets)

I have seen too many directors of children's theatre (who once studied with Sally Struthers or went to high school with Cher) promise the world to the kids and, on opening night, deliver a plastic rubber ball.

"And then, when the prince rescues the princess, we'll have a forty foot tower which will hydraulically open and reveal a multilevel set with glass chandelier and a forty-seven foot staircase covered with red velour".....Says this director as the children gather at his feet, their eyes sparkling as they envision this glorious set.

Then, on opening night, these kiddies run to the theatre to discover the set is actually two steps leading up to a platform set before a black curtain. The director will shrug and say, "Oh, don't worry. We'll use our imagination."

Look. I like you. I never lied to you.

THEN DON'T LIE TO THE KIDS!

Have your set designed early and know exactly what it will look like before sharing it with your actors.

Yes, you will have to make concessions as the deadline approaches, but be realistic from the start and explain exactly what you expect the sets to look like to your young thespians so they too can imagine.

By planning your sets early, you will know how much room the Pumpkin Goblins will have to dance or how high the platform for the Spirit Of Safety will be. You will be able to point out during rehearsals that a young actor will be standing **on** a rock at this scene and for him to remember, so on opening night he doesn't stand BEHIND it!

Do not depend on the sketch that comes in the back of some scripts. It may have been great for the theatre it was designed for, but if you are doing it on the floor of the cafetorium, will the original Broadway set look as impressive?

Face facts. You are going to have to have a set designed that will work for your group. The best way to do this is to know what you want.

WHAT WILL YOU NEED?

First reread the script.....yes, again! This time, keep an eye open to the number of sets (scenery) needed. You have chosen a script that has a minimal number of changes as I told you way back at the beginning, right? Good for you. Now reread and see if you can combine any sets. A door to a palace could be played before the main curtain, assuming you have a curtain. Or it could be done using the real door to the auditorium. Does Cinderella really have to go from inside the kitchen to her garden to get the pumpkin? Why not have her have one on hand (a can of pumpkin sauce?). See how many scenes you can get in one set.

Now, start doodling what you imagine it to look like.....I know. I know you can't draw a picture of a full moon.....I'm only asking you to do some rough sketches so your set builder knows where you want the grand staircase and where you want the stove.

As you sketch, be whimsical. Add a flash of color here or a dash of panache there. Trees in fantasy-lands don't have to be green (unless you have pulled them from your stock sets). Large colored flowers, like the kind you make to pin on wedding cars, can easily be glued to the bushes and trees for add color (and to fill up a stage).

Be aware as you doodle that wood costs money and a whole forest of orange tress could be suggested by only three. Be realistic in drawing and know if your stage crew can make the transformation from Billy's bedroom to "a place on Mars" within twenty seconds.

BE CREATIVE, BUT CAUTIOUS

Remember, this is a STAGE PRODUCTION. It is not TV and does not have to be totally realistic. Use suggestive sets as well. A grouping of platforms with bright colors and a few suggestions of sets can make a wonderful looking "Wonderland".

A door frame braced and a hanging window frame can make the suggestion of a house as long as the actors don't "walk through the walls". These suggestive sets also help in reducing the time between set changes. Parents tend to lose interest in a play that has fifteen set changes, each one requiring five minutes.

Be aware of things that must work on your set. In other words, will a door have to be opened and closed? (It's easier to just paint a door on a set than have it practical.) Will the window shutters have to work? Will the trees have to sway? The house to sustain a tornado? A fence be able to take the weight of three children? All these problems must be identified before the sets are constructed.

Also keep in mind the amount of furniture you are doodling. Keep it simple. A chair and a table indicate a kitchen. No need to build a refrigerator, a sink with a disposal and a china cupboard unless they are a vital part of the story. (In which case, I would tend to ask, "**Why** did you choose that script?")

Combine sets with curtains, if you have them. One set can be elaborate, another just a suggestion. You may want to keep entire areas empty for the crowd scenes or if you plan to have the rhythm band march on to perform. Don't clutter your stage with things you don't need.

SET CHANGES

As you doodle your sets on paper, remember that these will have to be removed by your stage crew, which may very well be two "older" boys. Make them lightweight.

Also, be aware of your cast size. You do not have to build full size sets when your actors are half sized. Build to their specifications. A house that is four feet high looks full size when your actors are only three feet tall.

The horrible reality of the situation is that most royalty plays and children's classics have many set changes. Try to design many of your sets with two sides so a change can be made as the audience watches. Try to eliminate as many blackouts as possible. Watching the toy soldiers change "Billy's Bedroom" around to become "The Enchanted Forest" adds to the fun of the theatre.

As you take pencil to paper, remember your proposed "blocking". Will an entire marching band fit through the one door of the castle? Will the audience be able to see the wolf hiding, if there is a huge tree center stage? Will the tap dancing number have to be cut down because some dummy (that is, you) put a huge platform center stage?

LAYERING YOUR SETS

The quickest way to make set changes is to "layer" your sets. This may cut some of your available acting space, but can help alleviate the problem of your audience falling asleep between scenes.

If you are lucky and have a stage, there should be two sets of curtains on it, the front (proscenium) curtain and a middle curtain that divides the stage in half (lengthwise).

Why not start your play in front of the first curtain (if there are no crowd scenes), open up the curtain to reveal the second scene and then for the third scene, open the middle curtain? Try to use sets more than once in each scene.

For example (refer to scene illustrations beginning on page 75), assume you are doing the children's play, "The Wizard Of Oz". Your script calls for:

Scene 1: Dorothy's House in Kansas

Scene 2: Munchkinland

Scene 3: A cornfield

Scene 4: The forest

Scene 5: Another part of the forest

Scene 6: Oz's Palace

Scene 7: The Witch's Castle

Scene 8: Oz's Palace

There are eight scenes with seven different sets. Reading your script, you realize that scene four ("The Forest") and scene five ("Another part of the forest") can be combined. Good for you! You've cut down one set change already.

You also realize that scene one ("Dorothy's House in Kansas") has little action except for Dorothy and Toto singing, "Over The Rainbow". You decide to put that scene IN FRONT OF YOUR MAIN CURTAIN. Since the scene is little more than a prologue, you decide to have the house on stage and perhaps one stalk of corn to show it is a farm.

During the tornado, as the lights flash and the curtain is opened, the house **remains on the stage.** (The cornstalk is taken off and the witch's legs are placed under the house.) Your new set is played BEFORE THE MIDDLE CURTAIN on your stage. A cut out of hills and a fence brightly painted make Munchkinland come alive.

As Dorothy sets off on her trip, the lights dim and the house is removed along with the fence. Two brightly colored trees are added and perhaps your corn stalk is brought back in. Suddenly you are in scene three with no hesitation. The cut-out hill remains on stage.

For scene four and five (your combined forest scenes), move your hills to one side and center your trees, all played before the middle curtain.

The reason you have played all this on half the stage is you have a permanent set built behind all these drapes. It may be your most elaborate, or in this case, the one that most of the action takes place on ("Oz's Palace").

When it comes time to arrive in Oz, the curtains open and all the sets up to this area are taken off. You have an elaborate throne room with various levels (since you can use platforms here and not have to move them).

For the witches castle, a short scene but with a lot of characters (if you include flying monkeys, etc.), close the middle curtain and use a suggestive set.....(pot boiling, a table, perhaps a window).....and have all these portable to move back to Oz once again.

As you can see, playing area is cut down and the director must be aware of this when blocking the play. Most times, "layering" your sets can help eliminate a lot of wasted time. However, don't layer your sets if your scenes really require a lot of room. If fifty munchkins are planned on being used, perhaps limiting your stage to half its playing area wouldn't work for your group.

Try to lead up to a "big set", hopefully, the finale of your show. This could be a dazzler and send the parents home thinking they saw more than they did.

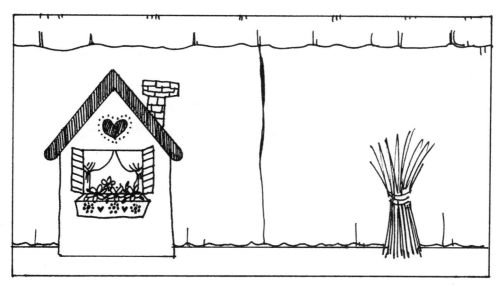

SCENE 1 – Dorothy's House In Kansas
Played before Main Curtain with minimal sets.

SCENE 2 – Munchkinland
Played before the middle curtain. All sets are freestanding cut-outs, brightly colored.

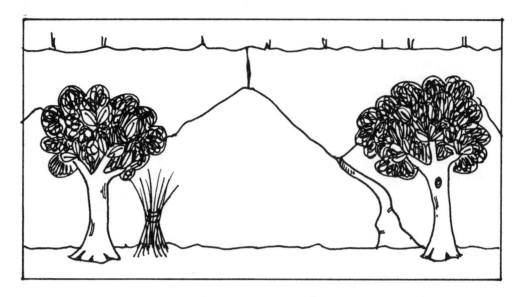

SCENE 3 – A Cornfield
House and fence removed. Trees and cornstalk added.

SCENE 4 – The Forest & SCENE 5 – Another Part Of The Forest
Trees moved to center. "Mountain" moved to one side, yet still visable.

SCENE 6 – Oz's Palace & SCENE 8 – Oz's Palace

The "Big One"—using the entire stage. The set is non-moveable and is hidden throughout the play by the middle curtain. Platforms can be used and permanent back walls. It does not extend past center stage, although props can be brought in during set change.

SCENE 7 – The Witch's Castle

Just a few props placed before the middle curtain. By now your audience is so "into" the play, they don't mind a suggestive set for a short scene.

WATCH THOSE BRACES

A point to remember as you are sitting there with your Magic Markers, creating the best set design since "Camelot", is that your sets must be able to stand up! Allow room for braces to insure your castle walls don't come tumbling down. Also, be aware that your set will have braces when blocking your scenes. Come dress rehearsal, young actors invariably trip over the braces, adding an "earthquake" effect to your "Candy Queen's Castle".

MORE IDEAS

If the idea of free standing sets is too much for you or your budget won't allow all the lumber it will cost to make five different sets, why not take a clue from the old fashion "mellerdrama" days and have your sets painted on large sheets of paper or on curtains that can then be flipped like on a giant sketch pad? Then, all your chairs, cupboards, etc., can be painted right on the backdrop to look three dimensional.

Not old enough to remember "mellerdrama"? Well, surely, you've seen those old "I Love Lucy" programs where she and Ethel put on a play ("The Wednesday Afternoon Fine Arts Club Presents....."). The sets for their shows always look like real sets for a low budget show. But they are clever! All the scenery was painted on curtains that could be changed, thus saving time. Even when they put on "extravaganzas" (Ricky promised to sing and foot the bill, no doubt), the sets were cute and easily moved. Next time Lucy comes on, watch for those old sets. ("Steal from Lucy"? Well, if you're going to steal.....steal from the best!)

If you have completed your sketches and they look like ka ka (that's a technical term for "yech"), do not hesitate to run to the library and look at some illustrated children's books. See what you can borrow from these books. Scale the background down to a usable, make-able portable set for your show. Many are beautiful and you must set your goals a little less high than what you see, but it will give you an idea.

Once you've finished your "renderings" (doesn't **that** sound impressive, Mr./Ms. Show-Biz?), you may want to take another hard look at your budget. Your dreams of a 12th Century Chinese Temple may not match your $2.47 budget.

Remember.....simplify at all costs!

But never feel cheated. For no matter how much your sets cost, whether it is made of aluminum foil and chicken wire or from the finest canvas on the most durable lumber.....Whether it was designed by you or a real artist.....Whether it was built by the shop class or a master builder.....One thing will be true for all the sets: They all seem to fall during at least one performance!

So, now aren't you glad you made your sets lightweight and inexpensive?

Chapter 13

"DANGER.....CONSTRUCTION AREA"

(Building Your Sets)

One of the great thrills about theatre is the illusion. (Not DIS-illusion, although you may run into that half way through this venture.) The entire art form is a fraud.

Out in Los Angeles, if you go on the Universal Studio Tour, you find out that a killer shark is a robot, the motel room in "Psycho" was a fake and even King Kong looks phony close up! (I personally was crushed to find out that the Cleaver residence and Dr. Welby's house, although one and the same, was not a real house at all!) Nothing is what it seems.

So be it with your sets as well. A wall does not have to be a wall. It can be simply a flat. (I know that is a technical term so I will repeat it slowly.....F-l-a-t.)

FLATS

A flat is aptly named because it is, you guessed it, flatto! It is usually made of canvas stretched across a wooden frame. Scenery is painted on it and several strung together can make an entire room that a child of four can lift (or, more than likely, knock down).

You can make your flats out of old bed sheets or cardboard over a frame. Try to keep your flats no bigger than 6ft x 4ft. You can always lash a few together to make a bigger set, but any bigger, they tend to be unmanageable.

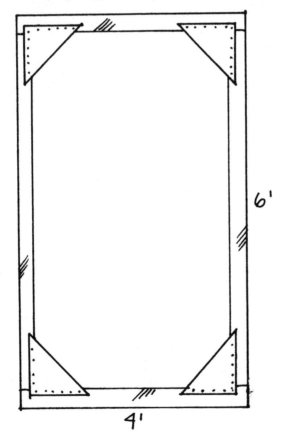

Backview
(no braces yet)

Sideview
(Note braces are
attached on inside
of frame.)

Simply fasten a few pieces of wood together, cover with your sheet, using a staple gun to fasten, and paint. Make sure you have room on the back to attach a brace to make the thing stand up. (You can always have some of the older kids hold the set while it is on, however, the temptation to sneak a peek around it may be too much and your audience may be suddenly aware of a pair of eyes over your Castle of Versailles.

Using bedsheets, you may find that some paint soaks into the material. You may wish to consider using muslin or canvas for your set coverings. Cardboard is good because it is lightweight, but covering the flats with plywood, although making it secure, tends to make it too heavy for your stage crew to move.

For a large backdrop, such as the sky, dye your sheets and sew them together. You can sew on your hills, trees, whatever, using different colored sheets, if you don't want to paint them on. Then just hang the sheet on the back wall.

Stringing the sets together, you can lash them with rope or attach them together with hinges, making them a giant screen and able to stand by themselves.

You can get fancy and add shapes, if you so wish. Triangles for roof tops or turrets for castles can make your set look that much more real.

A cute effect can be made by having two sided flats with an exterior on one side and an interior on the other. When Snow White finds a little house in the woods, she can pull open the house to reveal the interior, like a story book.

Real doors can be made into the flats, but it is easier to have the kids walk around the flats than to hassle with cutting door frames and making doors that open and close.

ROCKS AND TREES

Trees can be cut out of heavy cardboard and braced to stand. Or you can build a frame and use muslin or canvas just like your flats. A fast neat trick for trees is to make them out of muslin, paint them, cut out colorful leaves (a good project for those not on the stage) and just hang them from the stage curtains. They can be pinned to the middle row of curtains and are easily removed by a simple yank. They also store away in a drawer, a plus for those of us who have limited space.

Rocks can be made the same way. Cut them out of cardboard and brace. If you need action to happen on them (the Pilgrims landing, for example) nail them to an old chair or stool. The rock can be huge, but if only one person will stand on it, no one will know that the rest of it is not "walk-able".

Large pillars or columns can be made from muslin and hung from the stage curtains, just like the trees. Painted to look like Promethius himself couldn't topple them, they give the illusion without the cost.

Three dimensional sets can be made out of paper mache and is a good project for older children. But for the most part, it is time consuming and messy. Cut-outs look cute and can set the mood of a children's fantasy even quicker than a realistic looking set. (See how good you've become at justifying?)

Also, using flats and not three dimensional sets can help you with your layered look. Putting a larger flat in front of a smaller one can make for quick changes!

SET CONSTRUCTION vs. SELF DESTRUCTION

Once you have met with your set constructor and given him your plans, do not feel slighted when he or she stares at them and mutters, "Very interesting", while holding them upside down. Simply remind yourself that YOU don't know the difference between a lathe and a hammer and laugh at the little jokes.

Your set person will take the plans that you have so painstakingly prepared and tell you not to worry. The sets will be delivered per your request.

NOTE: Worry!

With production weeks away and your crude drawings not looking too complicated, the set person will shrug and put the plans on his work bench before settling into a basketball game on TV.

I do not trust set people!

Make sure that you give this person periodic phone calls and make surprise visits to the workroom to see how the sets are coming. Prod him with promises like, "I'll give you a six pack of beer if you give me the Sugar Queen's kitchen".

Go and encourage his work. Do not stand there and look at his purple sky and orange grassy lawn and scream, "My God, I didn't know you were color blind".

Remind him (CONSTANTLY) of dimensions that you have given him. He may feel that a castle's turret should be taller than five feet but he doesn't know that it has to be hidden behind another set. A few inches here and there can add up to a set that doesn't fit your stage!

Usually your set person will delegate to a crew different parts of the set. Make sure that he is overseeing the entire project and that you're overseeing him. (Or her. Excuse the blatant sexism, but set constructors are usually helping daddies while costumers are moms. However, do not overlook anyone who knows their way around a sewing machine or a jigsaw! Good help is hard to find and all assistants who volunteer should be given equal chances to work on what they know best.)

THE KIDS BUILT IT!

Many directors think it would be fun to have the kids in the play build the scenery.

Many directors think that walking over hot coals can be fun.

Actually, having the actors help with the sets can be fun. Note I said, "help". To take a young actor, throw a hammer in his hand and say, "I need an enchanted island by three o'clock", can lead to emotional scars that may not go away.

However, working together to create a set is fun. You must budget enough time away from rehearsals to allow this.

Having a basic set built by a set constructor and having the kids help with the last minute items is the right way to go. They can make the flowers or cut the colored leaves out of construction paper while waiting for their cues. They can paint (OUTSIDE) some of the larger areas and construct some of the smaller flats.

The sets the kids build will not rival Broadway, but will be unique and lend a wonderful quality to your show. Just don't over burden them with building sets, learning lines, changing blocking and cleaning the theatre. They are kids.....Not your personal slaves, Cecil B.!

Make sure you allow time for "clean up" after a painting session and that you make sure that "good clothes" are never worn to rehearsal, especially if there is paint around.

You will be amazed at the creativity of some of your actors. Let them have at it and, although you may never have seen a lavender rocketship, enjoy their youthful enthusiasm.

Chapter 14

"BUT, SOFT! WHAT LIGHT THROUGH YONDER WINDOW....."
CRASH! ".....BREAKS?"

(Lighting)

If you are anything like me, you are frightened by the idea of plugging an electric hair dryer in the same room as a bathtub. All those stories I was told about people being electrocuted in their homes tends to make me walk about with a head of wet hair.

So, it comes as no surprise when I tell you that my basic rule for lighting the stage is this.....

DELEGATE!

There are actually people out there who can plug into more than one outlet and not cause a major blackout. There are folks who understand "kilowatts" and "dimmer switches" and can use these words in sentences.

I like my actors to be seen, but I think some children's theatres go a little overboard with lights, adding one more thing a child can be nervous about. Have you ever seen a Little Bo Peep, played by a third grader, walk out on stage and freeze when a ten thousand watt spot light hits her? It's a wonder she doesn't confess to shooting the principal!

What was once a nice cozy stage for rehearsals is now a glowing platform surrounded by a sea of darkness. The children are suddenly squinting, hoping not to fall off the edge of the stage as they grope about trying to find their way off. Pretty scary stuff for a child whose mother won't let him watch horror movies on cable TV!

Keep your lighting plot simple and make sure you will have time to rehearse your young actors with all the lights. Most children's pageants or plays do not require a great deal of complex lighting tricks. A simple "Lights up" at the beginning, perhaps a bit dimmer at the scary parts and then "Go to black" at the end can be just what you need. Don't try to get tricky your first day out!

YOUR LIGHTING PERSON

You are getting tired of going to the copying machine to run off extra scripts for your staff.....I know! I know! But it is important that everyone of your staff members has a script of his own. This includes, from the beginning, your lighting person.

Even if all you want is "full lights up" through the entire production, let your lighting person have a script. He or she may have some ideas as to lighting the play a different way, perhaps a bit more subtle in some sections, a bit bolder in others.

Spend time with your lighting person. Plan to meet at the beginning of rehearsal and go over the equipment that is on hand. If you are lucky, your school auditorium will have the following:

A DIMMER BOARD

This is usually located in the wings, right off the stage. It is the control board that operates the lights that are, hopefully, hanging up on your grid. There are big dimmer boards and small dimmer boards. Your dimmer board may be portable and operated from the back of the house (with miles of cables running through the audience) or may be built in and ancient.

A dimmer board has, on first glance, thousands of small, sliding knobs that control all the lights. (Usually they control more than what you have, so don't worry about all the switches.) By sliding the knobs up, the lights come up. By sliding them down, the lights dim. All the lights are attached to this and it is important that you and your lighting person review the board to know what is operatable and what is not.

LIGHTS

In most theatres, these are large, black tubes with what looks like a porch light inside. Your lighting person will mutter, "Looks like you've got a couple of bad Fresnels here". Don't let it throw you.

The two types of lights you probably will encounter are Fresnels and Ellipsoidal (Leko) lights. **Fresnel** (called so because of its Fresnel lens—Clever, no?) throws a softer type light without the hard cut edges other lights throw. **Ellipsoidal** are used for longer "throws" and can be focused to a finer point. They usually have funny wings on the side of the spot to help adjust.

These lights are moveable for the most part. They can be "re-hung" in various formations to light your playing area.

You should have at least six Fresnels to light the playing area from above and six Ellipsoidals to light it from out front. Hopefully, your lighting person will know your stage and what areas to light.

CABLES AND EXTENSION CORDS

You will need miles and miles of thick utilitary lighting cables and extension cords, if your lights are not permanently mounted. Do not plan on going home, grabbing the extension cord from your clock radio and racing back to school to plug in your lights. NO!

The extension cables you need must be thick, heavy industrial cables. If you are using portable lighting, these cables may be running through the house (taped down securely, of course) and having a fire start on one of these lines tends to upstage your play a wee bit.

During your lighting rehearsal, you will have the playing area strewn with cables as each light is checked, focused and positioned. You may not want kiddies around during this, so plan to have a rehearsal with just you and your lighting person.

SPOT LIGHT

This is the epitome of show biz to most people. When they see this, they know they have come to the "theatah". It is used to emphasize certain areas of your stage and is excellent for special effects. If your school doesn't have one, no problem. If you do have one, do not overuse it. Do not plan on using a spot light as your prime source of light. Spots throw a high powered beam of light and the object of the light can get uncomfortably hot. Use it sparingly and at moments of highest impact.

Using two spots can eliminate some of the harsh shadows that one spot can produce. By crossing the lights, the actor is bathed in the light. However, this is twice as hot and will require two extra hands since a moving spot is not usually controlled by the dimmer operator.

GELS

Lighting is used for more than just allowing your audience to see their little darlings. It can set a mood by the use of colors. The way lights achieve this coloring is gels. They are colored pieces of acetate that can be slipped over the lights to color your stage. Using "white" lights only can give your stage the aesthetic quality of a prison break. The use of colors can soften the lighting. Using colored gels on your lights, you can mix the colors to give the impression of a soft white light without the harshness to audience and cast members.

Basically, red, blue and green lights are used to create a soft white look to your stage. When one color is used more than the other, a mood is established. (Example, dimming the red and green lights, the blue light becomes your primary source and the effect becomes one of nighttime.) You can use a variety of other colors or shades to fit your basic needs.

FOOTLIGHTS

These are the strip of lights that are at the foot of the stage (assuming you have a stage, of course). They look very theatrical and help you for one specific reason.....Children rarely fall off a stage when there is a row of lights between them and the orchestra pit. If you do not have footlights, do not worry. It is one less thing for your to have nightmares over. If you do have them, use them, if you wish. A very scary effect can be achieved by lighting the footlights and dimming the overhead lights, giving the actors the resemblance of ghosties who hold flashlights under their chins to scare little brothers.

These lights are usually permanently colored red, green and blue and sometimes can be folded right into the stage, if you need more playing area.

PLANNING THE LIGHTING

Once you have taken inventory, set up times for your lighting person and you to meet and discuss what effects you wish to achieve. Perhaps you might want to give them one rehearsal time to just run through the lighting cues (if you insist on going "Broadway" with this project). This is called a "cue to cue" rehearsal and may be just you and the lighting crew for a rehearsal block. During this time, you, with your script in hand, will do a "one person" version showing the lights where each person will be right before and after a lighting cue. It is done pretty fast as you dance around the stage yelling out things like: "The house lights dim and the stage lights come up after the overture. There are three kids over her, stage right and a house front down center. They do three songs with the lights staying the same until the Ugly Troll enters from down left on page fourteen. Dim the lights here and give the Troll a spot. That stays the same until page nineteen where we have the tornado effect....."

All the while, you will jump around, becoming the Troll or the house or whatever, just so the lighting crew will know where the effects come and what to light. (Of course, prior to this you have given them the majority of their cues and they have it written down as well. You are basically just reviewing the essentials for them.)

"Cue to cue" rehearsals are boring for you. It comes at a time when you will have a million and one things to do.

That is why we revert back to rule one and SIMPLIFY. Have lights, yes. Have a difficult lighting plot, no. Besides, with all the instamatic cameras flashing, no one ever notices the lights anyway.

Chapter 15

"WHAT IF YOU GAVE A SHOW, AND NOBODY CAME?"

(Publicity)

You have spent eight weeks in a room with seventeen children who insist that the height of intellectual humor is knock-knock jokes. You have typed up and duplicated more scripts than were used for the entire run of "Hello Dolly". You have given up evenings to paint an enchanted forest and ruined your best sneakers in the attempt. You have lost your appetite for anything that remotely smells like fast food after endless evenings of grabbing a burger on the run.

After all you've done "for the good of the show", you deserve someone to come and see your production!

You shouldn't have much trouble getting your star's parents and grandparents to come to the theatre (loaded down with four video cameras, several still cameras and a tape recorder). However, if you want the community at large to come to your show, you must spread the word. Even if you only want other classmates to attend, it is imperative you get the show on the road.

After all, Veronica Volunteer only has so many relatives she can drag.....Ooops, I mean who are dying to see your production of "Santa Claus Goes Latin". You **will** need a Publicity Chairperson to spread the word.

YOUR PUBLICITY PERSON

If you are going community wide for auditions, you will need your publicity person on hand even BEFORE you start rehearsals. They will be responsible for getting out the word you need actors and actresses.

It is one of the easier production jobs that parents will be clamoring for, as they rarely have to come to a rehearsal or spend hours sewing sequins on the Blue Fairy's dress. Grab a parent who can write an acceptable grocery list and plead with them to spend a few minutes at the typewriter on your behalf.

The first course of action is, of course, to plan ahead. (This coming from a man who has yet to send out his 1985 Christmas cards!) Make sure when putting together your rehearsal schedule you have included when publicity should go out.

There are any number of ways to publicize your event. Creative Publicity Chairs will think of lots of ways to get your play in the headlines. However, the most effective are:

    PRESS RELEASES

    PHOTOS

    POSTERS/FLYERS

PRESS RELEASES

These are the backbone to your publicity campaign. Whether you are sending them to the New York Times or to the editor of the school's daily bulletin, your press releases will contain all the information anyone would want to know about your "Valentine Day A Go-Go" Program.

They are a simple, double spaced TYPED one page announcement of who, what, where, when and why. (We know the "how".....through a miracle of God!)

Press releases must be in the editor's hand a minimum or two weeks before you wish it published. (About a month before your opening night is a nice time to be mailing them out.) Of course, certain newsletters and local papers may have other deadlines, so be prepared.

Reminder: A daily or weekly newspaper does not have to print your press release. They may have enough news to fill their paper without worrying about your play. (Amazingly enough, to some people, your play is not front page material!) It is basically a public service they are providing. If you really want publicity in their paper, you can always take out a PAID ad which could run several hundred dollars. Better to contend with a press release which has a good chance of making it in for free.

LETTERHEADS

Get a copy of the letterhead of the organization sponsoring your play (get permission first!) then, by using rub on letters available at most stationery stores, put in bold letters across the top, "PRESS RELEASE". Duplicate several copies of this and you have an instant release form. (As an example, see the sample "PRESS RELEASE" on the "Happy Hollow Park And Recreation Department" letterhead that follows.)

If you can't use the letterhead, use the rub on letters on plain paper and type an address at the top. Or design your own "letterhead" using rub on letters and illustrations from those art books with copyright free illustrations. (As an example, see the sample "NEWS RELEASE" on self-designed "Acme Productions" stationery that follows.)

DATE

A date is always listed immediately under the Press Release banner. This is the date your release reaches the newspaper. It is important so the news editor knows your release is current.

IMMEDIATE RELEASE

On the left hand side, type IMMEDIATE RELEASE, if your release is ready to be printed. If you have specific dates you want the release to be done, you may specify it here in broad strokes. In other words, you can put the "shelf life" of your release here. (FOR RELEASE WEEK OF AUGUST 2-9.) Do not specify actual days you wish the release to appear. Editors hate that! A majority of press releases use "Immediate Release", so don't push it!

CONTACT PERSON

Directly across from the release dates, you should list a contact person and telephone number. This person should be able to give the paper more information regarding the play. This number is not printed so it can be a home number of your publicity chair or even your own number. Try to make sure whoever's number is used that that person is home during the daytime and can answer further details about the production. It should not be the number of the box office or some office that will not know what the paper is talking about when they call for more information (usually to check spelling, times, or perhaps to arrange a photo session! Lucky you!).

THE RELEASE

Begin typing your release half way down the page. Put a title to it but never fear about being creative here. Editors ALWAYS change the titles of press releases. Just put something to identify your release. ("Children To Perform Tragedy", "Temple To Host Variety Show", or just the title of your saga.)

Do not type your press release in all capital letters. You may think it looks like something Lou Grant would want, but it is a nuisance to editors to have to pencil in where the lower cases should go. Type it like a normal, double spaced letter.

Try to get most of the important information in the first paragraph. Editors are cold blooded when it comes to cutting stories and they may just edit your last four paragraphs without realizing the vital information is listed there. So, go for the Who, What, and Where in the first few lines. You don't have to be dull about it and you may even wish to start with an "attention grabber" as your seventh grade teacher always said. Just keep it short so the important information comes through.

Try to keep the release to one page. If you are going over one page, divide it between paragraphs and put "MORE" at the bottom of the page. At the top of the second page put the title of your press release and type PAGE TWO beside it. I can rarely think of a possibility where the release should be more than two pages, even with listing every kid in the cast.

At the end of the release, put either three asterisks or ### to indicate the end of the story. (You can also write -30-, if you want to feel like Brenda Starr, but that is a bit old fashioned.)

Check it over for typos and duplicate it with one for each of your local newspapers as well as a copy file for yourself. Mark on your file the names of the newspapers to which you send.

HAPPY HOLLOW PARK AND RECREATION DEPARTMENT
645 E. Sutton Lane, North Billingston, Ohio

PRESS RELEASE

June 25, 1987

IMMEDIATE RELEASE

For additional information:
Tom Beasley 549-3554

CHILDREN'S THEATRE CASTING

The Happy Hollow Children's Theatre Company will be casting their spring production "The Princess Who Didn't Drink Milk" on Friday afternoon, July 7, from 2 - 4 p.m. at the Elizabeth Taylor Junior High School Cafeteria, 574 E. Willow Street, Lakeside City.

The play, a comedy with music, needs four young girls between the ages of 7 - 15 and five young men ages 6 - 15. The play will be presented in September and all funds will go towards the elimination of world hunger. For further information, call Marion Hardgrove at 986-5574.

###

Acme Productions

540 Discovery Bay Blvd., Byron, CA 94514
(415) 634-5710

NEWS RELEASE

September 20, 1987

IMMEDIATE RELEASE

CONTACT PERSON:
Jody Amsterdam
450-5563

CHILDREN TO PRESENT PLAY

"The Tooth Fairy Versus Godzilla", a play about dental hygiene, will be presented on October 4 6 at the Edison Junior High School Auditorium, 56 West 9th Street. The original play with music was written by Dr. Lawrence P. Throckmorton and will be presented by members of the "Future Dentists Club". Curtain time is 7:30 p.m.

The cast includes Tyron Bradley as Mr. Tooth Decay, Chris Raymonds as Mr. Floss and Louise DeSimone as the Toothbrush. Others in the play are Billy Thomas, Carla and Sheena McCarthy, Tony Jarvis and Kelly Cartwright.

For ticket information, call 576-8889. All seats are 50 cents and all proceeds fight world tooth decay.

#

Mail these releases in business sized envelopes to all your local newspapers AT LEAST TWO WEEKS prior to the time you hope to have them printed. If you can, prior to the mailing, call the newspapers and ask who handles theatrical press releases. Try to get a name to address the release. Most newspaper people are less than thrilled to have a local junior high school teacher come down to the office to hand deliver such a release. (Chances are, you'd only see the receptionist anyway.) If, on the other hand, you know someone at the paper, use that contact. (Maybe one of your students or actors has a father or mother who works down there. Lucky you!)

You are not limited to the amount of news releases you give the paper and remember that they are not under any obligation to print your press release. Therefore, it is a good idea to follow up your press releases with other releases. You may hit a slow news day when the editor needs more copy to fill the paper. Spread several releases out over the weeks of rehearsal. The first might be the casting call, followed by, a couple of weeks later, an announcement of your stellar cast. Then, a few weeks later, perhaps one on the progress of your show and then, right before opening, a general press release with all the information in it.

HUMAN INTEREST

Keep an eye open for a human interest story as well. Do you have three sets of twins in your show? Is there a young actor who is related to a famous theatrical star of yesteryear? Are your costumes exact replicas of the original movie version? Are you using sign language as a part of the show? These are twists that interest newsmen and women to come out and perhaps do a feature story on your play. If you find something interesting, call the local paper and tell them. They may or may not agree with you, but it is worth a shot.

Do not limit yourself to just the newspapers either. Send releases to Senior Citizen's homes, college campuses, local theatres, any organization that has a newsletter, organizations your "stars" are associated with, and any radio or TV stations in your vicinity. (Don't overlook local cable TV companies! They love local interest stories!)

Blanket the city with these releases several weeks before your production! You will be lucky if you get them printed in large newspapers, especially if you live in a metropolitan area where your play is competing for space with an All Star Cast Revival of "Hello Dolly" down the street. But don't give up hope.

Keep mailing those releases in. If nothing else, think how your typing will improve!

PHOTOS

Having a photo in a newspaper is wonderful. The kids love it. Their parents love it and people actually look at pictures of little kids in cute costumes and may remember that you are putting on a show.

Do not expect your newspaper to drop everything to send a photographer down to cover your play. (You and I know it is front page material, but somehow, it is difficult to convince most editors that it rivals the latest peace talks.) YOU WILL HAVE TO HAVE IT DONE YOURSELF! (This comes as a surprise?)

Look around the merry band with which you have surrounded yourself. Surely one of those parents who you have beleaguered into working with you owns a thirty five millimeter camera. Someone must know the difference between an F-stop and a door stop. Grab them!

Set up a time, VERY EARLY IN THE REHEARSAL PROCESS, when you will take photographs. (This must be done right after casting in order to get the photos printed, duplicated and distributed.)

You are going to need an eight by ten glossy of two or three interesting looking characters from your play IN COSTUME! It should be sharp and close enough to capture the expressions of the children in the photograph. DO NOT take a photograph of the 134 member chorus or five kids standing there staring into the lens with those "School Picture"type grins on their faces. You want the viewing audience to see some of the excitement that your play promises.

Choose a couple of performers who will look good in their costumes for the photo. It does not have to be the leads and this is a good time to stroke those kids who are doing well but are less than stars. Let the costumer know which children you have chosen and what costumes you will need. The costumer should put these costumes on her priority list and begin to gather something that will pass for the costume. (If you have a costume closet from previous years, grab something that looks interesting and "in period" enough to pass. You don't have to worry about size since you can always pin it in the back.)

If you can get a set piece or some interesting looking background, by all means, grab it. If not, have the photo taken outside on a bright day against a blank wall. (It will look like a stage backdrop, if you stretch your imagination.)

Put your actors in an exciting pose that may (or may not) be in the play. Remember, your audience will not come with the newspaper in their hand, staring at the picture to compare with the actual action on the stage. You may have chosen two characters who never meet on the stage during your actual play, but who have interesting costumes. Try to get the picture from the waist up in order to capture the expressions of the young thespians emoting for all their worth. Use props from the show. Exciting sword fights look better than a princess staring off into space. If you are doing a classic show (Peter Pan, Snow White, etc.), try to get a picture of a scene everyone knows. (The witch giving Snow the apple, Mr. Toad in his car, Pinochio dancing.)

Once you get the photograph, run and get several prints made in 8 x 10 size to distribute to the newspapers. On the back of each, you should include a mini-press release that describes the action of the photograph.

You can type this on a slip of paper and tape it to the back of the photo. It should identify the people in the photo, their characters and the times and dates of the show. You can also accompany the picture with a press release. The photograph will probably not be returned, so plan on duplicating these for as many papers as you wish. (It might not hurt to make a couple of extra copies for your own scrap book as well as the scrap book of the young stars in the picture.)

The sharper and crisper the quality of the photo, the better chance it has of being printed. Do not rely on fuzzy instamatic-type pictures and DO NOT SEND COLOR PHOTOS to the paper! They will promptly be filed away under "hopeless".

8 × 10 PHOTO
Black and White

on back

EEEEK! Becky Thatcher (played by Mary Noonan) is less than thrilled with a gift from Tom Sawyer (Billy Stone) when Lakeside Children's Theatre presents "Tom Sawyer", April 14-18 at the Community Center, Room B. Showtime is 7:00 p.m. all nights. For tickets call Suzie Bradley at 895-3346.

POSTERS/FLYERS

Getting the word out is important! You will try every trick in the book to get someone to notice that you are putting on a show or pageant. You want them to know where, when, and what time! One of the best ways to do this is by making posters. After all, don't we all read billboards as we drive the highways?

Posters are very important if you are doing an "in-house" type show. That is, you are inviting only other members of your community, be it school or camp, with very little interest in attracting an outside audience. (In other words, you want the parents to come and that's it.)

Designing an attractive poster or flyer is important in this case, for that will be the chief means of communications to your potential audience. A great way to go is to have your cast members create posters and flyers. During rehearsal, have them draw on large pieces of cardboard a picture from the play. Use bright markers and heavy cardboard, if you want the signs to stand up. I like to use white poster board and often times, I have already had someone who has good printing to fill in the time and dates so the students just supply the artwork.

If you are planning on duplicating these childish scrawls, then only hand out BLACK markers on white paper. These are charming and it is a good idea for the front of your program as well.

If you are only going to use one of these "masterpieces", tell them that while all of them look great, you have to go with the one the printer thinks will duplicate the best. (No need to tell them that YOU are the printer.) Don't make this competitive. You might want to once again use this project to bolster the ego of someone who is cast as a "Banner Holder". Even if they aren't the star of the play, their program and poster cover is used. Pretty hot stuff to a six year old.

You might also consider using these drawings as the cover to your program. Again, make sure your young artists use bold black markers or dark ink. Have them draw their cover on ½ of a sheet of a regular sheet of white paper. Take the "most print-able" and have them printed on multicolored paper with the names of your cast inside. (See the sample "childish-type" drawing for a program on page 99.)

Another route to go is to once again corral a poor sucker.....Ooops, I mean a willing parent who has artistic abilities and have them draw a flyer on 8½ x 11 inch paper that can be duplicated. (Have them use one color ink.)

IMPORTANT INFORMATION FIRST

You must stress that on all posters the most important information is the name of the play, the dates and the time. Do not bury these somewhere amid a beautiful rendition of a 16th century mural. Get the name and the dates as pronounced as possible. Chances are, your masterpiece is going to end up on a refrigerator door as a reminder to mom and dad. They will want the dates to jump out at them so they won't forget little Samantha's debut as The Poisoned Mushroom.

Make sure each flyer and poster has the following information:

GROUP SPONSORING THE PLAY

NAME OF PLAY

LOCATION OF THE PLAY

TIME

DATE

MAPS, if needed, to a specific classroom or theatre.

See the following two sample posters/flyers, one with "childish-type" drawings and the other more sophisticated, on pages 101 and 102, respectively.

Camp Running Nose
presents
"Cinderella"

AUGUST 10, 1:30 p.m.
Community Center Auditorium
740 PIER AVE.
* FREE ADMISSION! *

CRYSTAL THEATRE CO.

presents...

A 1890's Revue...

AT THE

RECREATION CENTER

413 Jefferson Blvd.

AUGUST 10, 1:30 p.m.

✯✯✯
featuring
3rd, 4th, 6th. graders
and
talent, talent, talent

FREE ADMISSION
★Everyone Welcome!!★

★ REFRESHMENTS WILL BE SERVED ★

Once you have your flyer, bring it to your local instant printer and have them run off a lot in different colors. (Use your own definition of "a lot". I always find that for youth plays, 200 is a lot!)

Distribute them to your actors telling them to spread the word. Mail them out on your club's mailing list or to past students and actors. Post them on every available blackboard and bulletin board.

Canvass the neighborhood mall. Merchants are usually willing to post flyers in windows, if approached nicely. (And if the poster is attractive!) Promise them a couple of free passes, if they are not thrilled by the idea. (NOTE: Don't send your young actors out to do this! They tend to take a roll of tape and put up the signs themselves.....Usually over "Post No Bills" signs and movie posters. Be forewarned!)

Do not expect merchants to forgo their display in the front window for your poster of "Safety Week Pageant.....Starring Tom, the Stop Sign". He is doing it as a favor to you. Be nice and promise you will frequent his store.

OTHER PLOYS FOR YOUR PLAYS

There are many other ways to draw attention to your play:

1) Have a raffle for two winning tickets (free entry).

2) Hold a dress-up day when your young actors are given permission to go to their school in costume. (Arrange with both the principal and the costumer.)

3) Join local parades and march in costume.

4) Have your young performers do scenes at local malls or shopping centers. (A lot of time, they are desperate for entertainment! Check it out through the public relations office of the mall.)

5) If you are in a school situation, start by having mysterious clues about the play in your daily announcements or have a short scene put on over the loudspeaker one afternoon.

6) Try to get a tie-in somewhere. (Examples: If you are doing a "classic" story, have the library put up a display about the author. Or tie-in with a holiday celebration in your city or a parks activity.)

Remember, if you are doing a full throttle publicity campaign, you may end up with more audience than you anticipated. If you have only fifty seats (and forty kids in the play), don't do a media blitz!

You can plan on each child in the play averaging three people coming to see him. If you still need more audience, then by all means, hit the presses!

Just make sure you have room for the masses that will storm your auditorium to see "Thomas Edison Gets A Bright Idea".

Chapter 16

"ANOTHER OPENING, ANOTHER SHOW, ANOTHER BREAKDOWN!"

(Opening Night Problems)

You are coming down the homestretch! Opening night looms ahead, just a week out of sight. Your young actors are bored to tears rehearsing scenes they learned weeks ago. Your costumer is screaming she needs more time. Your set designer had an unexpected business trip to San Francisco, leaving your incomplete set out in the rain. The programs have been lost by the printer and a wave of chicken pox is going through the school, causing several of your leads to begin scratching. Your refreshment crew has decided to serve sushi on opening night and your parents call to tell you they can't come to the play because they are going on a cruise.

Did Gower Champion have these problems?

Take one crisis at a time. Do not get overwhelmed at all the work left to do. Believe me, the show will go on. It may be with fewer sets and less glamorous costumes than anticipated, but it **will go on.**

There are a million and seven problems that you are going to encounter on your way to opening night. I, of course, can list only one million and six for I guarantee that your problem will be so unique that it is unheard of in the annals of show biz.

Here, however, are a few you should be aware of as you start the homestretch run:

PARENTS

They will want to come to rehearsals or talk to you about little Irving's part ("It isn't a challenge to him. Last year he played 'The Little Engine Who Could' and now he's a tadpole!") or try to convince you to give their little darling the solo. STAY AWAY FROM THEM. Once in a great while you will come across the phenomenon of a parent who really is interested and want to help with no hidden agenda of getting their kid the starring role. Grab these parents. Keep your committees small and full of these types and your life will be happier. Be sure you ban parents from all rehearsals and tryouts. Children really are different knowing mom is out there, saying each line of dialogue with them.

PROFESSIONALS

You will run into people who once worked as an extra on "Days Of Our Lives" or was in the chorus of the third National Touring Company of "Annie" (fourth townsperson on the left) and they will want to help you more than anyone.

Try, in a nice way, of course, to get rid of these pests. Remember, this is not Hollywood or Broadway but a nice little recreational play. It is made to have fun and let the parents and kids have a good time. Professionals tend to stand over a cowering third grader and scream, "Ray Bolger never lisped, so young lady, neither will you". They also come with breathing exercises and "sensory memory exercises" that mean nothing to a child who only wants to remember which side the Duke makes his entrance from.

KIDS DROPPING OUT

If you don't vary your rehearsal schedule and make it fun, kids loose interest. Keep them occupied when they're not on stage by having them work on something related to the show.....Drawing posters or designing programs is fun. Make sure they are supervised while you are drilling the soldiers in their dance. Use what they make as much as possible and avoid "busy work" that will not see the light of the stage.

Kids do drop out for a variety of other reasons.....Grades have started to slip, basketball season starts, the family is moving away, etc. If they do drop, hopefully you will have enough time to bring up one of the merry villagers to learn the part or, horror of horrors, you may have to do it yourself. (Yes, **you!**) Don't make a big traumatic thing of it. The parents will understand why you are playing Hansel or Mr. Tooth Decay. Just don't ham it up too much. You can go on reading the script and most of the parents will think it is "delightful" anyway.

If you do move another child into the role, do not do it overnight. Make sure that child has enough time to feel comfortable in the role. Try to avoid "You-Are-Going-Out-There-A-Fourth-Grader-But-You're-Coming-Back-A-Star" type speeches as the poor kid will have enough pressure as it is. Let him or her carry the script on and read, if necessary.

If you lose several kids due to an epidemic, you may want to postpone the opening. You will have to notify all potential audience members and parents of the cast, but again, try to do it in a simple, non-hysterical way. Look on the bright side.....Maybe your sets will be done by then!

SETS NOT BEING DONE

So, you didn't check up on your set person and two days before opening you find a bunch of chicken wire and half sawn boards leaning against his garage. Don't panic. Go with what you can salvage. Do not complain to your actors that you will, "never trust Mr. Quigley to build your Lollypop Planet again". When you see your revised final set, coo with excitement and try to generate excitement with your cast. Ignore little Jerome's "I thought it was going to be painted!" comments and tell everyone that they will have to use their imaginations to get the audience to use theirs as well.

SETS FALLING DURING PERFORMANCE

No need to worry about this one. It will happen. Have several adults backstage ready to pick them up again. This is another reason why sets should be lightweight.

KIDS FORGETTING LINES

See "Sets Falling During Performance" above. This is another "given". Have a parent offstage with a script who can prompt them.

ACCIDENTS

There will always be accidents where there are kids. Know fundamental first aid and your liability. Keep an ambulance's number handy as well as emergency numbers for each child.

KIDS NAMES LEFT OUT OF PROGRAMS, COSTUMES NOT DONE, NO AUDIENCES, LIGHTS BURNING OUT, ETC., ETC.

This is YOUR fault. Haven't I told you to double check EVERYTHING? For shame! Now go back to page one of this book and start over!

YOUR OPENING NIGHT

It's here! The night of nights has arrived! You haven't planned so much for a single event since your wedding. It has finally arrived.

Close your eyes for a second. Take a deep breath. Now imagine yourself on the day of your big opening. See yourself totally relaxed as you call in sick to work so you can have the day all to yourself. Imagine soaking in a hot tub, having a leisurely lunch with close, intimate ADULT friends at your favorite bistro. See yourself doing some window shopping, finding the perfect outfit to wear when the audience starts shouting "Director! Director!". See yourself calm and relaxed as you know all systems are go and all problems have been solved.

You may as well imagine a romantic interlude with the sex symbol of your choice as you are daydreaming.....BECAUSE NONE OF THE ABOVE WILL COME TRUE ANYWAY!

Oh, you may call in sick to work, but it will be the truth. You may find yourself sick with worry. Don't panic. Put things in perspective. In ten or twenty years, the children in the play will be grown and very few people will be around to remind you of your debacle. (I'm only teasing. I know you will be great!)

There will, of course, be last minute crises that spring up so prepare yourself for them. Programs may need to be picked up, costumes may need to be dropped off, the auditorium may need to be swept out. Now, aren't you glad you took my advice and got a few assistants on board? And when your assistants call to say they have to work that day, just roll up your sleeves and start to work.

OPENING NIGHT DAY

During the day of your opening night, try to get to the theatre, if it is open, to double check that your set is still up, your seating arrangement is made, your auditorium's house is clean. Check that the refreshments will be able to utilize the refrigerator or kitchen or whatever your refreshment crew will need. Run a sound check and a light check, if you can get your committee heads there to assist. Be sure the piano is there and tuned, if you are going to use it.

It is always amazing in community halls and school auditoriums that a piano that has been there since the Eisenhower years will suddenly disappear on the day of your "Spring Sing".

Try to make a quick check of everything during the day of your show, especially if you share the facility with other groups. That way, if the girl's volleyball team has moved your set that morning for a big game, you have someone to go to and scream. Remember, very few offices are open after five and you may have no one to call to find out what happened to your Big Rock Candy Mountain set that was there before the senior citizen's bingo tournament.

Using your lunch hour to make a quick "look-see" is smart because it will give you a few hours to get things back to normal should things not be where they should be.

OPENING NIGHT NIGHT

First and foremost.....EAT DINNER!

This will make a difference on your outlook for the evening ahead. A starving director is a cranky director and you may not be able to view the play in the correct perspective while your stomach growls through the first act. You have suffered enough these last months so indulge.

Arrive at the theatre two hours before the performance is to begin (if you have made sure that everything is in its place). Have your committees there also. You should have:

MAKEUP CREW (One to four parents, depending on cast size)

HOUSE CREW (Ushers, ticket sellers, house manager)

LIGHTING CREW (Two or three)

COSTUME CREW (Two or three)

SET CHANGERS (Two)

BABYSITTERS (A few)

This last category is needed if you are running actors from a classroom down a hall onto the stage. You will need "sitters" to watch as each group awaits its turn. Usually in school pageants, each class is playing a different part of the play (Tin soldiers are third graders, Lollypops are second graders, etc.) and they must wait in their classroom for their big moment. Have parental or teacher supervision for these groups lest you call "places" and they are all discovering where the absent teacher leaves her gradebook and making changes.

Each of these crews should have been versed in what their actual jobs are and should go right to work with little instruction from you. You have had as many as possible at your dress rehearsal and they are aware of what is needed to be done.

They should set up in anticipation of the young actors to appear. The makeup room should be a place that has access to running water. The costume crew should have an area where last minute patching can be done (and electrical outlets are available for last minute pressing). The lighting crew should be testing all the lights and the prop crew should be making sure all props are available.

If you do not have the luxury of all these crews, you and your assistant will have to run like mad to make sure everything is in its place. It can be done with a minimal crew, so don't panic.

An hour before the production time, your cast should arrive. Prior to this, you should have stressed the importance of arriving on time. You will find that some of them will be there when you arrive to unlock the theatre while others will arrive five minutes before curtain breathlessly screaming, "My dog had puppies right before we were going to leave!"

(A note home to the parents advising them of drop off time is important and should go home a couple of weeks before show time.)

As the children are dropped off, your "house" should be open, for the majority of parents are not going to go home and then turn around and come back.

Either have someone greet the children and take them backstage (declining mom and dad's offers of help so they can sneak a few pictures backstage) or do it yourself. In any matter, the parents should be shown to the auditorium or snack bar BUT SHOULD NOT BE ALLOWED BACKSTAGE. (If they didn't volunteer for a crew when you needed them, you can do without them now. I always find that the story of "The Little Red Hen" seems appropriate here, but don't overload them with children's stories.)

BACKSTAGE TRAUMAS

Your cast will be hyper.

Change that to: "Your cast will be **very** hyper".

Have them change into their costumes and go to the makeup crew for their makeup (providing you are using makeup). Have games available for them to play.....Correction: Have QUIT games for them to play. Leading them in a rousing game of "Hide and Seek" is a definite no-no. Card games, board games, coloring books are all wonderful ways to occupy their time.

Do not stand over them and give them last minute changes as if it were opening night on Broadway. ("OK, Delmont, drop your speech on page fourteen, make your first entrance from upstage right instead of down left, change the flower bit to be a water glass shctick and drop pages nine through seventeen inclusive.") You must give them the impression of total calm. (Talk about your acting!)

For the most part, your children will be calm and enjoying it all. However, there is always one or two who saw "Forty Second Street" on TV and will walk around going, "Oh, I'm so nervous! I hope I don't forget my lines. Is my costume all right? My opening prop! Where did I leave it? Oh, please a glass of water. I must do my voice exercises!" (You think I'm kidding, don't you? You just wait until **your** pint-sized Tallulah starts emoting.)

Nervousness is as contagious as the measles. Try to keep your little star away from the others. And, while on the subject, don't YOU make them any more nervous than they are.

STORY TIME (AGAIN): I went to a children's play where I knew a lot of the young actors. I snuck backstage to see how everything was going (something as a director I would never allow someone else to do) and asked the director, who was new, where the star of the show was. The director blithely answered that, "Our little Cinderella is in the bathroom throwing up", and then she went back to filling the other children's minds with thoughts like, "Everyone will be watching you!" "You must be good tonight for your parent's sake," etc., etc.

Move over, Cinderella!

Don't make them upset. Remember, this is all a fun game and a good introduction to theatre. These little darlings are potential "stars" of tomorrow or at least future audience members for the theatre. Let them enjoy it.

Your crews should be running smoothly without you and you may find yourself a bit lost if you have done your job correctly. It will appear, if all is on schedule, that your job is done as makeup people rush by you for more water, the costumer is busy zipping kids into their kangaroo costumes and the lighting people are resetting the spot.

You may want to spend this time greeting parents as they arrive. It is a good time to hit them up for the next show and let them know how important it is to get involved "for their little Sunny's sake".

SHOW TIME

Try to get the show started as close to your time as possible. You might want to hold the curtain for five or ten minutes until late comers are seated, but no more.

Make a final check with the cast that everyone is where they are suppose to be, that they are all being supervised, costumed and made-up. Send those crew members who have finished their job out into the audience to keep backstage as clear as possible.

You may want to start by saying a few words yourself. As the house lights dim, you can step before the curtain to greet the parents and thank them for attending. This always smacks of grandstanding to me, but then, I just hate standing on the stage while 200 parents murmur, "That's the one who keeps sending all those letters to us, begging us to work!"

Step off and let the overture (if you have one) begin.

This is it! You've done your job and now it is up to your young thespians to put it across.

If you are truly a remarkable director (one who is ready for the "Little Theatre Director's Hall of Fame"), you will have enough assistants backstage so that you can sit in the house and watch what you have wrought. But do not plan on this! More than likely you will be needed backstage to keep everyone quiet and things running smoothly.

REMINDER: No one likes a hysterical director backstage. Keep your calm and help others keep theirs and things should run smoothly.

Above all, enjoy your success. Aside from a shaky video tape one of the parents is taking, your opening night will soon just be a memory. Enjoy! You deserve it.

YOU DID A GREAT JOB!

Chapter 17

TAKE YOUR BOWS

(Curtain)

Congratulations, again. The show is over and you're being held aloft by grateful parents who recognize your genius. Even Veronica Volunteer is speechless (although she will regain her vocal ability to make a long, boring speech at the next P.T.A. meeting at what a marvelous "group effort" the play was, conveniently forgetting to mention YOUR name!).

Don't let it go to your head. You still have a few details to handle as your cast runs out to their various parties.

Make sure that the rooms you have used have been returned to their normal state of cleanliness. Have a time when your scenery will be removed and know where you will store it. ("A garage somewhere" is not specific enough.) Gather up all costumes and send them to the dry-cleaners **before** storing them (again......Where?). Clean up all the spilled punch, makeup and paint that has found its way onto the floor.

In short, return the area back to the way it was before you made it "what it is today".

I realize you are an adult and are responsible, but theatre has a bad enough name as it is with school and recreation leaders. Leaving a room looking like the "A-Team" used it for combat practice does not endear you to the administration. You want them to realize how beneficial this theatrical experience has been for the children and not think about the cost of a new floor for the gym (where one of your over-enthusiastic set builders nailed a two by four).

You want them to see only a sparkling production and not all the pitfalls that went before it. You want them to sing your praises and to bask in the thank you notes from happy parents who will support any future theatrical endeavors that may be planned. You want them to realize what a terrific job you did when they are choosing a director for next year's show.

What?

You want to do this again? You want to put up with all the screaming parents, the set builders who run out of blue and paint the sky orange, the costumer who buys sixty yards of plaid material that clashes with any color know to man, the custodian who takes special pleasure in locking you out of your rehearsal room?

You want to put yourself through all that again next year? You really want to become a director for children's theatre all over again?

You better believe it!

THE END

! DRAMA WORKSHOPS/CONSULTATION !

Contact the author directly for workshops and/or consultation for your group.

Write:

John Carroll
P.O. Box 4061
North Hollywood, CA 91607

....

! FREE CATALOG !

Send **for free** catalog of *INNOVATIVE CURRICULUM GUIDEBOOKS AND MATER-IALS* in MOVEMENT EDUCATION, SPECIAL EDUCATION and PERCEPTUAL-MOTOR DEVELOPMENT.

Write:

FRONT ROW EXPERIENCE
540 Discovery Bay Blvd.
Byron, California 94514

Questions? Call 415-634-5710